ASSESSING LEARNING

Standards, Principles, and Procedures

Urban Whitaker

with a Foreword by Morris Keeton

cael

Council for Adult and Experiential Learning
226 South 16th Street
Philadelphia, Pennsylvania 19102

Table of Contents

Foreword

In the CAEL literature on assessment, this book replaces Warren Willingham's *Principles of Good Practice in Assessing Experiential Learning*. From the time of its first appearance in 1977, Willingham's book was "the Bible of prior learning assessment." Actually it dealt as extensively and as explicitly with the assessing of all learning that occurs away from campus as with that which occurs prior to matriculation. In practice, however, the *Principles* was largely unused among those evaluating the learning outcomes of internships, cooperative education, and practica. At the same time a growing number of practitioners of prior learning assessment have accepted the *Principles* as the canon of good practice.

Willingham's monograph has been largely ignored by the assessors of classroom-based learning. Its key principles apply as cogently and as helpfully to the assessment of normal collegiate instruction as to learning and competence derived in any other way by learners. But it has been little used in this more extensive domain.

During the twelve years since the *Principles* first appeared, much has been learned about the specific problems and opportunities encountered by competent, conscientious assessors as they seek to understand and recognize what learners have learned. New tools have been invented to help learners to articulate what they know and can do and to clarify their claims to creditable achievement, to help assessors improve the reliability of assessment, and to save assessor time. The CAEL literature has gradually accumulated this knowledge of improving practice and new tools. But nowhere, prior to Simosko's 1988 book, had this information been brought together in a single place, organized for the convenience of users, and reflected upon as to its wider potential utility. With the Simosko handbook in place, there remained the task of providing a systematic explication of underlying standards and principles. This book by Urban Whitaker meets that need.

A further consideration prompted the commissioning of this book. New levels of demand for improved assessment practices have arisen within the past three to five years: first, for improving admissions and placement of the growing numbers of adult learners re-entering education, and second, for greater accountability to taxpayers and consumers as to the learning outcomes of college programs. For postsecondary educational institutions to respond to these new levels of demand, they need the kind of explication of standards, principles, and guidelines which this book provides. A particularly troublesome aspect of the surge of enrollments by adults 25 years and older has been the increase of incompetent or unethical purveyors of "credit for life experience" programs and services. These schemes have become a rip-off of the learners and a serious obstacle to efforts to gain legitimate and fair recognition of learning among the workforce and other mature learners.

CAEL set to work in 1987, in response to these needs and dangers, to develop a set of written materials that would capture the new state of the art of assessing learning and competence. Susan Simosko, in 1985, had written for CAEL a guide to learners on identifying their creditable learning and documenting their claims (*Earn College Credit for What You Know*, Acropolis Books). In 1987 she was commissioned to edit and help write a new handbook for faculty who serve as assessors (*Assessing Learning: A CAEL Handbook for Faculty*) (CAEL, 1988). At about the same time Urban Whitaker was asked to develop this companion monograph, *Assessing Learning: Standards, Principles, and Procedures*. No one supported more strongly than did Warren Willingham the move to develop this successor to his earlier work.

I cannot overemphasize the relevance of this book to the assessment of what students learn in the normal course of college and university studies and of employer-managed and entrepreneurially run training and education programs. The *standards and principles of good practice* in assessment are the same, wherever and however the learning takes place. As the first of the cardinal standards herein stated says, experience *per se* is not to be substituted for *documented learning assessed by competent, objective experts*. Whether the experience is in the classroom, on the campus in the laboratory or studio, on the job, or in an intensive hi-tech training program, different learners learn differently from these experiences, and the only sound basis for giving recognition for learning is the assessment of the actual learning and competence achieved.

For this reason I hope that academics and trainers everywhere will take seriously the need for valid and reliable assessment of the learning outcomes of their work. A teacher or trainer who does not know what students are gaining from the instruction or training provided is also unable to plan intelligently to improve instruction. But, almost as important, if a school, college, or university offers programs for which there is no reliable, periodic assessment of learning outcomes, the institution is in no position to offer a guarantee of the value of its credentials whether they be certificates, degrees, or licenses to practice.

There is a division of labor between this book by Urban Whitaker and the others in the new CAEL literature. Whitaker restates and clarifies standards and principles for which the Simosko handbook (while drawing on the Willingham statement of principles) provides tools and processes for implementation. Some of these tools and processes are briefly treated in this book; but that treatment is provided in order to clarify the standards and principles. The Simosko book uses the principles to illuminate the need for appropriate applications, but is intended primarily to be a handbook for practitioners. An additional book, focused on portfolio-assisted assessment of learning, edited and co-authored by Elana Michelson and Alan Mandell, will appear later in 1989 as a further complement to the Simosko and Whitaker books.

At the date of publication of this book, CAEL has had a fifteen year history and has undergone one change of charter and two changes of name. CAEL began as a three year project (1974-1977) of the Educational Testing Service (Princeton) under the name "Cooperative Assessment of Experiential Learning." Upon completion of that initial three-year research and development effort, CAEL began to operate under a new charter as a free-standing association of colleges and universities named the Council for the Advancement of Experiential Learning. In 1985, to reflect the emerging implications of its initial commitments, CAEL again took a new name; viz., "Council for Adult and Experiential Learning."

Of all those who have contributed to the work of CAEL through its fifteen year history, no one has taken a wider range of responsibilities nor kept up a more encompassing concern for the whole of CAEL's mission than Urban Whitaker. Many adherents of CAEL have been interested solely in its work on *prior learning assessment*. Others were interested almost exclusively in CAEL's work in fostering the more widespread and more astute use of hands on experience in collegiate instruction, as in internships, practica, and cooperative education.

Still others "came aboard" only after CAEL began to pay special attention to eliciting greater responsiveness to adult learners on the part of education providers. This last group has been relatively uninterested in CAEL's assessment services or in its agenda of enhancing instruction through first hand experience. Urban Whitaker, however, has kept all of these concerns in balance and in fruitful interplay. It is, accordingly, a particular pleasure to see this work of his mind and hand come to fruition and to express a determination that the book will receive the widest dissemination which CAEL can obtain for it.

> Morris Keeton
> President, CAEL
> March 15, 1989

Preface

This Preface has two purposes: (1) to answer the question, What is the *authority* for a book that moves away from merely stating "principles of good practice" to describing "standards of excellence" in the assessment of learning? and (2) to acknowledge the major contributions of the many colleagues who have helped to prepare this book. The two subjects are thoroughly interrelated.

Authority. CAEL's work in identifying the **standards**, principles, and procedures described in this book began with the state of the art as it existed in the early 1970's. A strong foundation for the present commentary was built during the first three years' work in CAEL (nee: Cooperative Assessment of Experiential Learning) which were devoted to development and validation of new assessment resources. That project was initially funded by the Carnegie Corporation, with later help from the Ford Foundation, the Lilly Endowment, and the Fund for the Improvement of Post-secondary Education. The project culminated in the publication of Warren Willingham's *Principles of Good Practice in the Assessment of Experiential Learning* (1977). Willingham combined into one publication the research results of 26 CAEL books, monographs, and research reports. In the following decade the *Principles* book was used by thousands of assessment practitioners and by all of the regional accrediting bodies. It influenced the development of new roles for experiential learning and served as a guidepost for quality assurance.

Our "authority" for moving toward a new rigor in quality assurance comes from two years of intensive conversations with hundreds of learners, assessors, faculty, administrators, and accreditors. We have tapped into the experience of the past by interviewing professionals in every phase of the assessment process. All of the members of CAEL (now the Council for Adult and Experiential Learning) and NSIEE (National Society for Internships and Experiential Education) were invited to share in the development of this commentary. Both organizations included this revision project on the agendas of their national conventions, which resulted in valuable contributions to the development of a new statement of **standards**, principles, and procedures.

The "authority" of these faculty and administrative practitioners was leavened effectively by the invaluable participation of all six regional accrediting associations and COPA (Council on Postsecondary Accreditation). The combined contribution of their experience, insight, and concern constitutes an authoritative basis for the establishment of a new quality assurance framework for the assessment of learning. I must emphasize, however, that neither the authority cited above nor the acknowledgments noted below should be construed as "approval" of the contents of this book. I have respected the judgments of those consulted. I have borrowed liberally from their insights. I acknowledge the fact that the strengths of this book rest on the contributions of numerous professional commentators. I took very much to heart the advice of one senior accrediting commission officer who said, "Don't try to please us, don't try to write a consensus—just get all the advice you can, and then write what you think is right." That is what has been done. Many are to be thanked for what is useful in this book. I alone must answer for what is not.

Acknowledgments. This successor to Warren Willingham's *Principles* was first suggested by **Ralph Wolff**, Associate Executive Director of the Western Association of Schools and Colleges (WASC). His constructive comments at a panel discussion sponsored by CAEL in 1986 were a significant contribution to this work. **Warren Willingham** agreed that the time had come for a "more rigorous" statement of **standards**, and his comments were very helpful in developing the first draft outline for this book.

Of the many colleagues who have contributed to this project I want to express special appreciation to those who reviewed the entire manuscript and made major contributions at various stages of its development: **Leah Harvey** (Metropolitan State University, Minn.); **Martin Thorsland** (Empire State College); **Paul Jacobs** (Thomas Edison State College); and **Jane Permaul** (UCLA). Each of them reviewed the book in penultimate draft and provided detailed and very helpful, page-by-page annotations.

Henry Spille, **Sylvia Galloway**, and **Eugene Sullivan** at the American Council on Education reviewed the drafts of several sections and offered very useful detailed suggestions.

James Harrington and **Catherine Marienau** shared with me some helpful "principles of good practice" prepared for The Alliance: An Association for Alternative Degree Programs for Adults.

Arthur Chickering's sharp insights and **Grover Andrews**' wisdom and experience were especially helpful in developing the first draft and in polishing the list of **Ten Standards**.

I relied heavily on **Jane Kendall** and **Garry Hesser**, along with many colleagues in NSIEE who added great strength to the sections of this book that deal with sponsored learning.

I received special help from **George Bates, Bessie Blake, Paul Breen, Harriet Cabell, Philip De Turk, Arnold Fletcher, Jackson Kytle, Terri Hedegaard, Larry Lujan, Bill McDermott, Betty Menson,** and **Peggy Upton**.

Jean Whitaker not only helped with developing many of the perspectives that shape the text, but offered the creative environmental support that is essential to the completion of any long term writing project.

From the original suggestion to the final minute of proof-reading, **Morris Keeton** has been the primary source of the inspiration and creative evaluation that have attended this two year project. A respected friend and trusted mentor for many years, Morris has never run out of time and willingness to help when I have sought his advice. That has been often. This book would not have been completed without his major contributions. Whatever its strengths prove to be, they all prospered from his counsel.

To those many friends and colleagues whose names I haven't mentioned here, please know that I appreciate the help you have given to the completion of this work. I feel much more like a committee chairperson than a sole author. This book is a collection of insights from the experiential learning community. When it serves well, it will be to the credit of many, many contributors. When it stumbles or fails, it will be because I have not accurately translated their experience and wisdom into effective **standards**, principles, and procedures for assessing learning.

(U. W., San Francisco, Jan 20, 1989)

Ten Standards

For Quality Assurance in Assessing Learning for Credit

ACADEMIC STANDARDS

   I. Credit should be awarded only for learning, and not for experience.

   II. College credit should be awarded only for college-level learning.

   III. Credit should be awarded only for learning that has a balance, appropriate to the subject, between theory and practical application.

   IV. The determination of competence levels and of credit awards must be made by appropriate subject matter and academic experts.

   V. Credit should be appropriate to the academic context in which it is accepted.

ADMINISTRATIVE STANDARDS

   VI. Credit awards and their transcript entries should be monitored to avoid giving credit twice for the same learning.

   VII. Policies and procedures applied to assessment, including provision for appeal, should be fully disclosed and prominently available.

   VIII. Fees charged for assessment should be based on the services performed in the process and not determined by the amount of credit awarded.

   IX. All personnel involved in the assessment of learning should receive adequate training for the functions they perform, and there should be provision for their continued professional development.

   X. Assessment programs should be regularly monitored, reviewed, evaluated, and revised as needed to reflect changes in the needs being served and in the state of the assessment arts.

Chapter One
Definitions, Propositions, and Assumptions

All of us are lifelong experiential learners. That we are is a compelling fact. The question is not *whether* there will be experiential learning, but how effective it will be.

Because of this basic truth, two priorities arise for educators: (1) "learning how to learn from experience" emerges as a major objective of education—at all levels; and (2) achieving the right blend of experiential and traditional classroom learning activities—to fit each individual's learning style—becomes a daily requirement for educators and other facilitators of learning.

These two educational priorities are being met unevenly. Although neither is the primary subject of this essay, both are appropriate starting points for considering the assessment of learning.

"Learning how to learn from experience" is not an easy task. It is made more difficult by the fact that doing so is only rarely recognized as a primary objective. It is cited here because the process of assessment itself provides a primary opportunity for learning how to learn. The assessment of prior learning (in a sense, all assessment is necessarily of *prior* learning) is an essential part of successful planning for future learning. It offers both process and content information to assist new learning: awareness of the strengths and weaknesses of the learner's style helps to plan improvements in the learning process; and identifying the quantity and quality of the past learning provides a content analysis that is an essential foundation for setting new learning objectives.

The blending of experiential and traditional classroom learning is not a new phenomenon. It has been done, and done well, in many cooperative education, internship, and other field and laboratory programs for a long time. But the assessment practices in some of these programs are inadequately developed. And the rapid growth in experiential learning activities of all kinds has added urgency to the need for new statements of assessment **standards,** principles, and procedures.[1]

Traditional Learning and Experiential Learning

We have chosen "Assessing Learning" rather than "Assessing *Experiential* Learning" as the title for this book. We did so because the rules for assessment are essentially the same for all types of learning. To learn is to acquire knowledge or skill. To assess is to identify the level of knowledge or skill that has been acquired. Acquiring learning and assessing learning are interdependent processes. It is particularly important to realize that assessment, undertaken creatively, promotes additional learning.

The distinction between "traditional" or "classroom" learning and experiential learning is an *input* rather than an *outcome* distinction. James Coleman has analyzed the differences (he refers to the traditional process as "information assimilation").

Differences Between Experiential and Classroom Learning (paraphrased from James S. Coleman)[2]

INFORMATION ASSIMILATION (classroom learning):

1. receiving information (through symbolic sources such as lectures or reading);

2. assimilating and organizing information so that a general principle is understood;

3. applying the general principle in specific instances;

---

[1] Joan Knapp and Paul Jacobs have suggested that, "An important distinction must be made between assessment and setting standards for assessment. Assessment is the process by which experiential learning is identified, evaluated, and equated with an amount of college credit. Setting standards for assessment refers to the process of establishing the criteria against which experiential learning is to be evaluated to determine whether it is adequate, worthy of college credit." *Setting Standards for Assessing Experiential Learning,* p. 2. (See Reference #8 on p. 103.)

[2] Chapter Five, pp. 49-61 in *Experiential Learning: Rationale, Characteristics and Assessment.* (See Reference #7 on p. 103.)

4. applying the general principle in new circumstances.

EXPERIENTIAL LEARNING:

1. acting and observing;

2. understanding the effects of the action in a specific instance;

3. understanding the general principle;

4. applying the general principle in new circumstances.

The most important difference cited by Coleman is the *source of information*. In traditional learning the source is "symbolic"—such as listening to lectures or reading. (But note that both are also *experiences*.) In experiential learning the source of information is "acting" or "observing;" that is, something the learner does, or watches as somebody else does, rather than something heard or read about.[3]

According to Coleman, the difference in the *source* of information leads to a vital difference in the learning *process*—more deductive when information comes from traditional sources such as lectures or libraries, and more inductive when information comes from acting or observing action.

These distinctions are useful, but their utility is in the process of *acquiring* learning, not in the process of *assessing* it. The essential difference is in the education input, rather than in the learning outcome.

David Kolb implicitly acknowledges that all learning is experiential.[4] Calling his work a theory of experiential learning, he incorporates so-called "traditional" inputs into his learning cycle, processing them as *reflective observation*. This analysis, of course, can be done

[3] Morris Keeton and Pamela Tate have defined experiential learning as "learning in which the learner is directly in touch with the realities being studied." They go beyond Coleman's definition to suggest that, "experiential learning typically involves not merely *observing* the phenomenon being studied but also *doing* something with it, such as testing the dynamics of the reality to learn more about it, or applying the theory learned about it to achieve some desired result," *learning by experience – what, why, how* . (See Reference #6 on p. 103.)

[4] Kolb identifies four elements in the experiential learning cycle: concrete experience, reflective observation, abstract conceptualization, and active experimentation. (See Reference #4 on p. 103.)

with any experience: listening to a lecture, reading a book, watching someone else's action, or actually doing something. But, again, the differences are *input* rather than *outcome* differences. They are vitally important in *planning* for learning; they are barely relevant in *assessing* the learning outcomes.

Learning: Teacher-Directed, Self-Directed, Undirected

At first glance it appears that Coleman's traditional learning is *teacher*-directed, while his experiential learning is *self*-directed. It would be very neat to extend the thought further and identify three combinations of authority and activities in the learning process:

authority	*activities*
teacher-directed	traditional learning: classroom, lectures, library
self-directed (but campus-monitored)	sponsored experiential learning: internships, service learning, cooperative education
undirected	prior experiential learning: life and work experience

These descriptions are neat. It is instructive to ponder them. But they are not really accurate. There are elements of all three types of direction (authority) in all three types of learning activity.

Traditional learning may be the purest of the categories in the sense that it is so often a primarily teacher-directed activity. Ideally it would be only incidentally and temporarily teacher-directed, the self-directed learners having consciously opted for professional help to supplement a personal long-range plan. "Teacher-directed" would be a tool used within a basically self-directed learning process. Undirected, serendipitous learning no doubt occurs, in varying amounts, to supplement the other results.

Sponsored experiential learning, such as cooperative education and internships, should not be, and usually isn't, purely self-directed. The degree of preparation and site supervision varies a great deal. Sometimes more is left to self-direction than ought to be. However, even when there is minimal preparation and there is no site supervision by the campus, there may be varying degrees of teacher-direction, ranging from *none* in the most permissive arrangement, to *complete direction* by a teaching-oriented (but not campus-connected) work supervisor.

Finally, even with *prior experiential learning* the degree and source of the direction may vary. A candidate for prior learning assessment may present a background of almost purely undirected (virtually un*planned*) learning from a variety of life experiences. However, especially where work experience is involved, it is likely that the learning has been significantly facilitated by others; e.g., job supervisors or trainers.

All kinds of learning are mixed in terms of the sources and degrees of direction. Multiple direction is common. Whether in a traditional classroom setting or on-the-job, the learner is likely to have help from various sources in directing the learning process. Teachers, supervisors, fellow students, fellow workers, friends, relatives (and even casual acquaintances in brief conversations) can suggest new or revised learning goals or activities. Ideally the use made of these various sources of help should be controlled and organized by the learner. Self-directed learning—including timely decisions to seek directive assistance from others—maximizes the opportunity for effective formative evaluation. Teachers, supervisors, and other formal facilitators of learning cannot be in continuous attendance. Only the learner is always there, always in a position to recognize new directions for effective learning.

The Assessment Process

The relationship between the direction of learning and its assessment presents two temptations that often lead to serious errors in assessment. First, and most seriously, there is the temptation to confuse educational inputs with learning outcomes. The most common instance of this error in classroom learning is the inclusion of "seat time" (attendance) in the determination of grades (and, hence, of credit). (See Chapter Six for a more detailed discussion of this problem.) In sponsored experiential learning this error surfaces when internships are evaluated in terms of "hours per week." The same error is often transplanted into portfolio evaluation of largely undirected or self-directed prior learning, by the forging of some inappropriate equation between "years of experience" and "units of credit." In all three cases the error is the assumption that *time spent* leads to *learning acquired*. When credit is granted for input rather than for outcomes, the assessment process is short-circuited and credit is given for experience rather than for learning.

A second problem, particularly with teacher-directed learning, arises from the temptation to overvalue the directing facilitator's personal conception of the learning *objectives*. For example, in a course on Twentieth Century History one instructor may emphasize social history, another political history, and another economic history. While the institutional objective (and perhaps the learner's) may be a balanced and general knowledge, the individual instructor's concept may be quite different. The assessment is warped accordingly. This second problem area is, of course, related to the first. "Assessment" is distorted by the learning director's inputs: determining the content of lectures, choosing library assignments, approving particular internships or sites for work and learning, or evaluating the experiences described in a prior learning portfolio.

Effective assessment is enhanced by clarity of learning objectives. In teacher-directed learning there is maximum opportunity for clear statement of objectives in advance of both the learning and its assessment. Unfortunately this opportunity is not always realized, as a glance at almost any college catalog will show: "A survey of American History, 1900-1950" is more descriptive of a possible learning *activity* than it is of any particular learning objective or *outcome*.

Rules for Assessing Learning

The first requirement for quality assurance in the assessment of learning is the identification of some rules for describing acceptable outcomes. The second requirement is to identify some basic practices that will lead to the sound measurement and evaluation of those outcomes. And, finally, we need to provide some guidance for developing local procedures to implement effective practices.

This sets up a three-tiered approach which is described in the title of this work as **Standards,** *Principles, and Procedures*. Recognizing widespread differences of opinion about the meaning of these terms, we turned to *Webster's Unabridged* to select appropriate definitions. We were guided by a firm determination to achieve quality assurance and maintain rigorous academic standards without losing the advantages of flexibility for experimentation and growth. We have sought to have the advantages of both rigor and flexibility by respecting the dividing line between ends (standards of quality) and means (general principles and flexible procedures).[5]

Among the many definitions of *"standards"* we have chosen the following as the best for this purpose:

> **something that is set up and established by authority for the measure of quality.**

Among other definitions of *"principles"* the following fits our scheme:

> **a general or fundamental truth; a comprehensive and fundamental law . . .**
> **a guide for conduct or procedures.**

Finally, Webster defines *"procedures"* as:

> **particular steps adopted for doing or accomplishing something.**

In summary, we have distinguished between the ends of instruction (the learning outcomes), the means to producing those ends (the educational "inputs"), and the ways to assess the learning to ascertain how effective the learning processes were. This book focuses on standards for sound assessment of learning outcomes. These standards state specific goals as to the qualities most essential to sound assessment. General guidelines for pursuing and reaching those goals are stated as principles of good practice. Practitioners are encouraged, further, to establish effective local procedures in applying those principles. These standards, principles, and procedures can together assure a high quality of assessment of learning whether the learning was acquired in the classroom or in the field, and whether its acquisition was teacher-directed, self-directed or undirected.

---

[5] For a similar approach, see *ETS Standards for Quality and Fairness* which "reflect and adopt" the *Standards for Educational and Psychological Testing* jointly issued by the American Education Research Association (AERA), The American Psychological Association (APA), and the National Council on Measurement in Education (NCME). The ETS adaptation of these standards comprises "both principles ... and policies that govern decision-making and guide the development of more specific goals. p. iv. (See Reference #2 on p. 103.)

Chapter Two
Standards for Assessing Learning

Two categories of **standards** are listed and discussed below. The first five **standards** are directly relevant to the assessment process itself:

I. Credit should be awarded only for *learning*, and not for *experience*.

II. College credit should be awarded only for college-level learning.

III. Credit should be awarded only for learning that has a balance, appropriate to the subject, between theory and practical application.

IV. The determination of competence levels and of credit awards must be made by appropriate subject matter and academic experts.

V. Credit should be appropriate to the academic context in which it is accepted.

The other five **standards** are related to the administrative context in which the assessment and the award of credit occur:

VI. Credit awards and their transcript entries should be monitored to avoid giving credit twice for the same learning.

VII. Policies and procedures applied to assessment, including provision for appeal, should be fully disclosed and prominently available.

VIII. Fees charged for assessment should be based on the services performed in the process and not determined by the amount of credit awarded.

IX. All personnel involved in the assessment of learning should receive adequate training for the functions they

perform, and there should be provision for their continued
professional development.
X. Assessment programs should be regularly monitored,
    reviewed, evaluated, and revised as needed to reflect
    changes in the needs being served and in the state of the
    assessment arts.

The primary emphasis in the discussion which follows is on
assessment for the purpose of awarding college-level credit. However, all of these **standards** are applicable to all types of academic
recognition of learning: waiver, advanced placement, and credit
awards. And most of these **standards** are equally applicable to secondary and postsecondary programs.

A. Academic Standards

Standard I. Credit should be awarded only for *learning*, not for *experience*.

This **standard** is, at once, the most important and the most
frequently violated quality assurance rule in the assessment field. It is
easier to quantify experience than it is to measure learning. But
experience is an *input* and learning is an *outcome*. Unfortunately there
is no guarantee that "x" amount of experience will yield "y" amount
of learning. The variables are numerous, including both the qualities
of the learner and the quality and duration of the experience.[1] Depending on the particular configuration of these variables there may be
significant learning from brief experience—and there may be little or
no learning (even regression) in the wake of long and intensive
experience. In fact, no "experience" is the same for all participants.
Two potential learners may sit through the same lecture—one a
motivated listener who learns something; another a daydreamer who
learns next to nothing. Two potential learners may put in eight hours
per week at the same work station—one who is ready to learn and
finds the environment intellectually exciting and challenging; another

---

[1] Morris Keeton has suggested that the learner is "a first key to quality assurance in
learning." He notes that, "Learners can guarantee outstandingly good or bad results
in many ways. If they are bright and eager to learn, they can absorb more knowledge,
pick up greater skills, and develop new perspectives and insights in ways that no
teacher could demand or coerce. Or if they are bright but rebellious or uninterested,
they can go through the motions of learning with astounding disregard for the
intriguing options to learn in their environments," viii, Reference #5 on p. 103.

who is baffled by the strange surroundings, or turned off by a personality clash with the work supervisor. And finally, for a variety of reasons, people react in a variety of ways to "life experiences"— some learn more, some learn less, and some seem to learn nothing at all from marriage, divorce, dealing with death, parenting and other personal and social activities.

An example from traditional classroom learning amply illustrates the error of confusing experiential inputs with learning outcomes. Giving credit for attendance in determining the course grade (unfortunately it *is* done) can result in course credit for the perfect attender who otherwise doesn't quite get a passing grade on the examinations. Conversely, some students who do get passing grades (low, but passing) may be denied credit as a result of poor attendance. The relationship between credit and learning is lost.

Some clear negative rules emerge: seat time, hours on the job, and life experience should not be calculated in assessing learning. They may be effective educational inputs, but they don't guarantee creditable learning outcomes.

The values of experience, *per se.*

While experience may not always be a source of immediate creditable learning, it may have other essential benefits. Requiring a particular amount of experience may be reasonable for some degree or certificate programs whether or not it has immediate learning results. Experience, *per se*, may provide a useful context for the application of past learning and effective guidance for planning continued learning. Experience also may be an important source of confidence and a necessary ingredient in making various career and personal decisions.

In summary, experience is good for many things. One of the best things about it is that experience is an excellent potential source of learning. But it is not, by itself, an adequate yardstick for assessment. The first and most important standard for quality assurance is that credit should be awarded—in the classroom, for internships, or in prior learning assessment programs—only for *learning*, and not for experience.

Standard II. College credit should be awarded only for college-level learning.

Although we will concentrate on the collegiate level, this rule could, of course, be stated more generally to apply to secondary as

well as postsecondary credit, and to either the graduate or undergraduate levels. In any case there are two questions about level that
must be answered before college credit should be awarded: is the
subject matter appropriate for credit at the college level and is the
learner's competence in the subject sufficient for college level credit?

Both questions are difficult to answer. These are "judgment
calls." Quality assurance in applying this **standard** comes primarily
from the application of the next three **standards**: requiring an appropriate balance of theory and practice; using only qualified experts to
make credit decisions; and requiring that credit awards should be
consistent with program goals. It is convenient shorthand to assume
that all three of these standards are reflected in the college catalog and
that, therefore, it is safe to assume that it is college level in terms of
content, if it is in the local catalog, or in that of any accredited college.
Unfortunately, catalog listings are not a reliable guide for identifying
college level learning. In some respects they are too restrictive, and in
other respects not restrictive enough. Using catalogs as "the standard"
limits the flexibility needed in some cases to serve legitimate individual needs and the practice stifles creative response to change. College
catalogs are also less than reliable guides to identifying the level of
learner competence that qualifies for college credit. This judgment
may be relatively easy for a subject like mathematics, and more
difficult for some of the social sciences and humanities. Even with
mathematics, however, there is overlap both in content and mastery
between high school and college. With foreign language, the confusion is much more serious. How should we view the difference, if any,
between high school Spanish 4 and College Spanish 1? How should
we respond to the fact that a high school student in Mexico may have
language mastery superior to that of a two or three term college
student of Spanish in the United States? And how do we decide
whether a speaking knowledge of Chinese (not in our *local* catalog)
might be college creditable? The rule could be: if it is in, or equivalent
to something that is in the catalog of *any* accredited college (Harvard's
for instance); and the learner's competence level is evaluated by *any*
qualified subject matter expert (not necessarily on our faculty), it is
college-level learning. In fact, however, not all catalog listings, even
those identified as applicable to degree completion, are acceptable by
consensus among colleges as identifying work of college level.

The **standard** is vital. College credit should be granted only for
college-level learning. But meeting the requirements of this **standard**

is necessarily a subjective process. Various principles of good practice will enhance the probability of quality assurance. **Standards III, IV, V** which follow provide important related safeguards.

Standard III. Credit should be awarded only for learning that has a balance, appropriate to the subject, between theory and practical application.

James Coleman suggests that, as exclusive sources of learning, both the traditional and experiential modes have predictable weaknesses. The common complaint about traditional learners is that, although they may have scored high on examinations about theory, they are weak when it comes to actual application. The common complaint about experiential learners is that they can *do* (in a particular setting), but can't *explain*—because they haven't really mastered the general principles that would allow them to apply their learning in new settings or to discuss the concepts embodying those principles in an analytic way.

In some subject areas (teaching and medicine are good examples) there is a reasonably clear distinction between the theory needs and the applied learning needs. In others (history comes to mind) it is more difficult to divide the learning on the basis of theory and practice. As we have phrased the **standard** above, we have used the qualifying language "appropriate" balance between theory and practice. The nature of the subject matter is critical and, again, the application of this **standard** is co-dependent with the next (the key role of experts in assessment for credit).

While the expertise of college faculties is essential to the successful application of the **standard**, that expertise alone does not provide automatic quality assurance. Since the expansion during the 1970's and 80's of experiential learning programs, a serious double standard has been exposed. Significant criticism has been leveled by traditionalists against experiential learning programs (particularly in prior learning assessments) in the form of an allegation that they fail to provide the necessary theoretical balance to qualify for the award of college credit. The complaint is often legitimate. This **standard** on balancing theory and practice arises just for that reason. Experiential learning should be balanced by enough theoretical learning to make it useful college-level learning. A common test is whether the learning is transferable to other contexts than that of the specific learning environment. For example, does the intern in an accounting firm (or a prior learner with "x" years of experience in the firm) know how to balance the books in only that one firm, or only when a particular brand of computer is being used? Or, does the learner know enough about the process of balancing books to use alternate equipment, or to move into another firm handling different accounts? Similarly, do the "A" students in an accounting class have all the learning necessary to *apply* the classroom knowledge in the workplace as successfully as they can pass exams on it in the classroom?

These are vitally important questions in the assessment of experiential learning, but they are just as vital in the award of credit for theoretical courses. The double standard masks serious weaknesses in the traditional curriculum. There are probably more theory courses where unbalanced credit is being awarded than there are internships or prior learning assessments reflecting the opposite problem. Only if the **standard** of balance is applied across the board can we be assured that we are maintaining academic quality.

In addition to an appropriate *balance* between theory and practice it is essential to leaven the mix with ample portions of *reflection* on it. The learning is not complete until the learner has some understanding of what both the theory and the practical experience mean. It isn't enough to have both in isolation; the learner needs to know why they are necessary and how each extends the value of the other.

There are many different ways of meeting this **standard** appropriately—on and off campus. In some cases, the balance may be achieved within a single course; in others it may be within a curriculum. There are numerous excellent examples of theory seminars related to appropriate practica. Thoughtfully developed internships can include "the right mix" of theory and practice in numerous ways. Even the assessment of prior learning may reveal appropriate balances achieved either through the direction of work supervisors or as a result of perceptive self-direction. Theory and practice can be related effectively on the job through reading, observation, and educational interviews.

In summary, the question should always be asked before either traditional or experiential credit is awarded: Is there an adequate "balance" between theoretical and practical learning?[2]

---

[2] Morris Keeton has suggested that "balance" should be put in quotation marks to emphasize the fact that the appropriate relationship between applied and theoretical learning is more complex than a simple balance. What should be sought according to Keeton is "a strategically effective interplay of theory and experience."

Standard IV. The determination of competence levels and of credit awards must be made by appropriate subject matter and academic experts.

Knapp and Jacobs have concluded that "consensus of experts is the primary mechanism for maintaining adequate standards." But, they have pointed out, "Standard setting is a highly judgmental process, with faculty or institutionally appointed experts at the center of the process."[3]

Two kinds of expertise should be brought to bear on decisions about credit. One is *content* expertise: how much does the learner know, and how well? The other is *academic* expertise: given the extent and quality of the learning, is college credit appropriate, and if so, how much, in what subject(s), at what level, and with or without the completion of additional learning?

Ideally, the academic and content expertise will be combined. One expert, a qualified faculty member, is able to make both decisions. However, when the subject matter is deemed to be appropriate for college credit, but is not included in the particular college's curriculum it may be necessary to consult outside expertise on content, while preserving the credit consideration for local academic decision. For this reason it seems inappropriate to require that credit decisions be made only by full-time faculty who are on regular appointment in the subject area. A shared decision—outside content experts on the level of learning and local academic experts on the amount of credit—preserves quality assurance while extending the institution's flexibility and range. It is similar to the extended range of service that one campus enjoys when it accepts transfer credit from other accredited institutions in subjects not locally taught. It is also the principle that permits colleges and universities to grant credit for CLEP, USAFI and ACE-approved assessments of non-campus learning whether or not the credited subject is taught on the campus.

Standard V. Credit should be appropriate to the academic context in which it is accepted.

There is no evident reason why this rule should not be applied to all learning regardless of its traditional or experiential sources. To limit credit for experiential learning only to certain aspects of the

---

[3] *Setting Standards for Assessing Experiential Learning*, p. 4. (See Reference #8 on p. 103.)

learner's program is to apply a double standard.[4] College-creditable experiential learning occurs in the major, in general education, and in electives. Provided that college credit is awarded only for college-level learning (**Standards I** and **II**) and that it has an appropriate balance of theory and practice in the judgment of qualified content and academic experts (**Standards III** and **IV**), the adequacy of its program fit should be determined independently of the source of the learning.

There are two reasons why particular care may be needed in fitting experiential learning to the certification context: *first*, experiential learning is often idiosyncratic and defies a straightforward connection to a course catalog or standardized test description; *second*, in the case of transfer credit, there may be significant differences between institutions in determining what learning fits what degree or certificate. Traditional titles for credited components often are not accurate descriptions for the individual learning outcomes of a particular idiosyncratic input. In such cases, where traditional, generally understood labels would not fully reflect the true nature of the credited learning content, it is necessary to clearly define and properly label the learning. This is crucial for the evaluating institution and in the event of transfer of credit between institutions. As course catalog descriptions are not available for such idiosyncratic learning components, the original transcripting institution needs to make clear the nature of the learning so that appropriate decisions can be made about potential duplication, overlap, and program fit.

B. Administrative Standards

Standard VI. Credit awards and their transcript entries should be monitored to avoid giving credit twice for the same learning.

In one respect, meeting this **standard** is a simple administrative matter. However, it may require academic judgment in cases where the relationships of the subject matter are complex or where credited learning has not been adequately described or clearly labeled. In any

---

[4] Jane Kendall has observed that, "It is ironic that experiential education—considered a suspect practice by many academicians until the last decade—is ahead of classroom teaching in proving its value for students' learning. But then innovations are usually held to a higher standard than traditional practices." *Strengthening Experiential Education Within Your Institution*, p. 74. Ms. Kendall is Executive Director of the National Society for Internships and Experiential Education (NSIEE). See Reference #10 on p. 104. See also Misconception #7 and Malpractice #8 in Chapter Six, below.

case, it is a decision that should be made *before* learning is undertaken (traditional courses or internships) or *before* learning is assessed and credited (in the case of prior learning). For that reason it should be a scheduled item in the process. When transcribing traditional courses, decisions ensuring against duplication are usually made in advance and built into the academic regulations. For prior learning assessment such clarifications and specifications need to be explicitly monitored to ensure conformance to standard registrarial practice.

Standard VII. Policies and procedures applied to assessment, including provision for appeal, should be fully disclosed and prominently available.

"Truth in advertising" is a vital element in quality assurance. Learners, accrediting agencies, other institutions, and the "consumer public" should know what rules are applied in assessing learning. It is important that the rules be comprehensive, explicit, and accessible. Every caution should be taken to avoid misleading statements that encourage unrealistic expectations.

Standard VIII. Fees charged for assessment should be based on the services performed in the process and not determined by the amount of credit awarded.

In traditional programs the cost of instruction, including assessment, is the same whether the student passes the course and is awarded credit, or fails and receives no credit. This relationship between fees and credit must be replicated in programs to assess experiential learning in order to preserve quality. Fees do vary as the amount of credit *attempted* varies. But fees must not be based solely on the amount of credit *awarded*.

Standard IX. All personnel involved in the assessment of learning should receive adequate training for the functions they perform, and there should be provision for their continued professional development.

This **standard** is as badly needed for classroom teachers and assessors as it is for experiential learning personnel. It has often been noted that college and university professors are better prepared in content than they are in process. The process training in most advanced degree programs tends to be for *research*. It might fairly be argued that most college and university faculty have had virtually no

preparation for their teaching and assessment roles, whether performed in traditional settings or for experiential learning. Even for
those who have developed appropriate assessment expertise for
classroom learning (usually through self-directed experiential learning), it is essential that professional development be provided in
support of any experiential learning assessment they undertake.

Each of the organizations listed in Appendix F has resources that
are useful for faculty and staff training programs.[5]

**Standard X. Assessment programs should be monitored, re-
viewed, evaluated, and revised as needed to reflect changes in the
needs being served and in the state of the assessment arts.**

Local review and evaluation can take various forms, including
academic and outside advisory panels. Nationally, there are numerous organizations that offer various kinds of assistance for monitoring
programs and assuring quality. There are three major organizations
devoted to different aspects of experiential learning. All have publication programs, regional and national conferences, and panels of
experts available to undertake local evaluations.

CAEL (Council for Adult and Experiential Learning) promotes
the study of all kinds of experiential learning and has a major commitment to quality assurance in the assessment of learning, especially
prior learning. NSIEE (National Society for Internships and Experiential Education) concentrates on sponsored experiential learning with
emphasis on internships and work experience learning. CEA (Cooperative Education Association) specializes in cooperative work experience programs. (See Appendix F for addresses and telephone numbers
for CAEL, NSIEE and CEA.)

---

[5] It is recommended that all faculty involved in the assessment of experiential learning
be provided with copies of *Assessing Learning: A CAEL Handbook for Faculty*. (See
Reference #12 on p. 104.)

Prologue
Chapters Three and Four

The **standards** described in Chapter Two are met in different ways by different institutions. There are general principles of good practice that enhance the likelihood of meeting the **standards**. Depending on institutional mission and personal goals of the learners there are many combinations of procedures that can be followed while operating within principles of good practice and seeking to achieve **standards** of excellence.

Principles and procedures for assessing experiential learning differ significantly depending on whether the learning is planned and sponsored by a postsecondary institution or is non-sponsored prior learning that is often the unplanned result of work and other life experiences.

The most important difference between these two types of experiential learning is that sponsored learning has the advantages of pre-planning. Both the setting of specific learning objectives and the selection of appropriate learning activities can be planned in advance. In addition, the measurement and evaluation of the learning can be anticipated and interwoven with the learning process.

These vital differences between sponsored and prior learning assessment have led us to treat them separately as we move from a discussion of **standards** (equally applicable to the two sources of learning) and begin a discussion of the principles and procedures that facilitate the maintenance of those **standards**. In Chapter Three we discuss the principles and procedures for assessing sponsored experiential learning. In Chapter Four we discuss the principles and procedures for assessing prior experiential learning.

For both discussions we have prepared *Assessment Charts* (see Tables One and Two) with three columns: *Column One* describes the six steps in the assessment process; *Column Two* comments on the division of responsibilities for each step; and *Column Three* relates each step to the **standard(s)** it is primarily designed to serve. [1]

The order in which these six steps are completed is not a firmly established pattern. Naturally *transcription* (*Step 6*) is the last step in both sponsored and prior learning assessment. And, necessarily, the setting of learning objectives can be considered in the assessment of sponsored learning but is essentially absent in prior learning assessment. Similarly the *documentation* step in sponsored learning can be planned as a supportive and integral part of the *measurement* step, while in prior learning *documentation* is largely retroactive.

In some respects *evaluation* (determination of credit amounts and grades) is the last step before *transcription* in the assessment of either prior or sponsored learning. However, in most cases of sponsored learning a significant part of the *evaluation* is done provisionally before the learning takes place. Most internship courses, for example, have projected credit values. *Evaluation* at the end is primarily to confirm (or deny) the satisfactory completion of learning objectives set at the beginning of the course. For courses in which letter grades (rather than pass/fail symbols) are to be awarded this aspect of evaluation is necessarily dependent on completion of the *measurement* step—i.e., judgment as to the relative quality of the outcome, not just the achievement of a specified minimum competence.

As the results of the assessment process accumulate they may influence the process itself. Unintended outcomes, in the case of sponsored learning, and unsuspected (and therefore unclaimed) outcomes in the case of prior learning, may alter the amount or type of credit that is appropriate. This is particularly important in the case of sponsored learning, as it may necessitate changes in the amount of credit that was projected for an internship or other experiential learning activity. The fifth step, *measurement*, may thus lead to revision of the third step, provisional *evaluation*.

Similarly, review of the learning outcomes may prompt significant changes in personal or professional goals, thus making it necessary to revise decisions made at *Steps 1* and *2* about fitting the learning to the learner's academic program.

Recognizing these interrelationships among the six steps it is

---

[1] For another commentary on the application of these six steps in the assessment of *sponsored* experiential learning, see John S. Duley, *Learning Outcomes: The Measurement and Evaluation of Experiential Learning*. PANEL Resource Paper #6, NSIEE. (See Reference #3 on p. 103.)

important to avoid a rigid, mechanistic approach to the process. All six steps are important. The order in which they are accomplished may vary with individual circumstances. It is advisable to approach the six steps as a checklist, leaving the question of order open to continuous review and crosschecking. The assessment process is dynamic and is, itself, an important source of new learning and new insights about personal and professional goals.

Chapter Three
Principles and Procedures for Assessing Sponsored Learning

The first two steps in the assessment of sponsored experiential learning are, in essence, the development of a learning plan. In *Step 1*, with the help of a faculty adviser the learner reviews overall long range goals and sets the context for experiential learning. Together the learner and the faculty adviser relate the planned experiential learning to the learner's academic program (**Standard V**). The learner also reviews career and other personal goals that may be served while fitting experiential learning to the requirements of the academic program.

In *Step 2*, again working together, the learner and faculty adviser identify specific learning objectives and the activities that will be undertaken to achieve them. It is at this point in the planning process that **Standards I, II,** and **III** are reviewed to ensure that the experiential activities will lead to college-creditable learning with the appropriate balance of theory and practical application.

In *Step 3*, the faculty member determines the amount of credit that may be awarded if the learning objectives of *Step 2* are met satisfactorily. As provided in **Standard IV** this is a faculty decision comparable to that made in classroom learning when the credit value of a course is identified in advance. As in the classroom, the credit is provisional; i.e., the actual award of credit is contingent on satisfactory completion of the planned learning. This step must necessarily be reviewed at the end of the process after the faculty member has *measured* the learning outcomes (*Step 5*).

In *Step 4, documentation*, the primary responsibility is with the learner to collect the evidence that the learning objectives have been met. The success of this step is facilitated by advance arrangements

Table One:
The Assessment of Sponsored Experiential Learning

STEPS	DIVISION OF RESPONSIBILITY	RELEVANT STANDARDS
1. ARTICULATION: Relate learning goals to academic, personal, and professional goals.	Joint responsibility of learner and faculty.	Standard V. (Learning must be relevant to academic program.)
2. PLANNING: Select appropriate learning objectives and activities.	Joint responsibility of learner and faculty.	Standards I, II and III. (Credit is awarded only for college-level learning with appropriate balance of theory and practice.)
3. EVALUATION: Determine the credit equivalency.	Faculty.	Standard IV. (Credit awards must be made by faculty.)
4. DOCUMENTATION: Collect evidence of learning.	Primary responsibility rests with the learner, but ideally is assisted by concurrent seminar or advising.	Monitor consistency with Standards I, II, and III.
5. MEASUREMENT: Determine the degree and level of competence achieved.	Faculty.	Standard IV. (These judgements must be made by faculty.)
6. TRANSCRIPTION: Prepare a useful record of results.	Administration with advice of appropriate faculty.	Standard VI. (Avoid duplication.)

with both the faculty and the site supervisor(s). Ideally a concurrent seminar (or at least periodic consultation with the faculty adviser) provides a continuing checkpoint. What needs to be checked is the effectiveness of the documentation in providing evidence that the learning satisfies the requirements of **Standards I, II, and III**; i.e., that it is college-level learning with the appropriate balance of theory and practical application.

Step 5, measurement of the learning outcomes, is the culmination of the assessment process. It is, per **Standard IV**, a faculty responsibility. It also is the final opportunity for ensuring that **Standards I, II, III,** and **V** have been met. At this time the faculty member determines whether the provisional credit projected in *Step 3* has in fact been earned. In addition, the possibility should be considered that some unintended (and possibly creditable) learning has also occurred. A full evaluation of planned future learning may also reveal changes in personal or professional goals as a result of the recent learning experiences. Finally, it is in *Step 5* that the faculty member needs to anticipate any necessary inputs into the transcribing process, *Step 6*.

The *6th Step, transcribing* the results, is primarily an administrative responsibility. In the case of scheduled internships and other regularly-offered field experience courses the process may be fairly routine—much like the completion of any catalog course. However, since experiential learning may lead to significant unintended learning outcomes, it is important for the faculty member to review the question of duplicated credit (**Standard VI**) and provide any information that may be needed for accurate transcribing.

The remainder of this Chapter is devoted to a more detailed discussion of the principles and procedures that support the **Ten Standards** of quality assurance. These principles and procedures are also summarized in the form of a checklist in Appendix A.

Step 1. ARTICULATION: Relate learning goals to academic, personal, and professional goals.

The fact that learning is determined to be college-level (*Step 2,* below) is not, by itself, a sufficient basis for granting college credit. In most instances the validity of counting learning for credit depends upon a demonstrable relationship to a defined degree or other program or course objectives. Completing this step is especially critical in planning individualized degree programs and in the design of institutionally sponsored off-campus degree programs.

In this first step, then, we will consider principles and procedures that bear particularly on achieving two standards of quality assurance: that the learning fits the program objectives (**Standard V**); and, as a part of that determination, that it has an appropriate balance of theoretical and applied components (**Standard III**).

Determine What Is Creditable	1.1 Each institution should have a published rationale for crediting particular types of learning in each of its programs. As program requirements respond to changes in the society and seek to serve unique needs of individual learners, institutions should have published processes for making exceptions or extending the rationale for determining what is creditable.
Seek Appropriate Mix of Theory and Applied Learning	1.2 There should be an institutional rationale concerning the most appropriate mix of applied and theoretical learning (**Standard III**), including how and when the two should be included in the student's educational plan.
Define Student's Learning Objectives	1.3 Student and institution should reach a clear understanding as to the general purpose of the learning activity and how the learning is related to degree or course requirements and the student's educational goals, including preparation for career and other personal and civic roles.
	1.31 It is important to use this opportunity to help students understand and choose learning goals that enhance self-awareness and personal development.
	1.32 Internships and other sponsored learning activities combine the necessity for increased learner responsibility with the

opportunity to develop the skills of self-directed learning and assessment.

1.33 Whenever possible, provision should be made for formative evaluation of learning progress. Students should be encouraged to negotiate new learning objectives if their experience so indicates.

Coordinate Goals and Site Selection

1.4 Care should be taken to identify learning sites at which learning appropriate to goals is a reasonable possibility. Students should have enough information to understand the pros and cons of alternate field placements in relation to learning objectives.

Step 2: PLANNING: Select appropriate learning objectives and activities.

Standard I dictates that only learning, not experience, should be credited. **Standard II** requires that only college-level learning should be granted credit by colleges and universities. These quality assurance criteria are more likely to be satisfied if careful attention is given to the planning of specific learning objectives that clearly differentiate between the experiential inputs and the learning outcomes. An important principle that helps to assure good practice is that field experience learning should not be undertaken without adequate preparation.

Determine the College Level of Learning

2.1 The following characteristics are often considered important in determining whether learning is of college level: (a) that there be a conceptual as well as a practical grasp of the knowledge or competence acquired; (b) that the learning be applicable outside the specific context in which it was acquired; and (c) that it fall within the domain usually considered appropriate to college credit as represented in the catalogs and practices of the colleges and universities.

Develop a
Learning Plan

2.2 To support the achievement of
Standard I (credit learning, not experience)
the learning plan should clearly differentiate between the experiential inputs and the
creditable learning outcomes.

2.21 Learning outcomes should be expressed as specifically as possible in terms
of the competences (knowledge or skills) to
be achieved and should describe the depth
or level of the competence and the process
by which it will be evaluated and measured. (See *Steps 3* and *5*.)

2.22 Learning activities should be selected
and planned for each learning objective and
in anticipation of the evaluation and
measurement steps in the assessment
process. (See *Step 3.6* on Learning Contracts.) One of the most important of the
learning activities is formative evaluation.
Periodic reflection to check on progress
helps to avoid unanticipated deadends and
to make any needed changes in the learning
plan. Both the teacher and the learner
should be alert to the happy possibility that
some unintended, but useful, learning may
occur. Thus assessment at the end of the
planned learning should also consider
unexpected learning results that may be
quite different from (and possibly even
better than) the intended learning.

2.23 Another helpful principle in finding
the most effective fit between the intended
outcomes and the selection of experiential
activities is that the learner's style might
well be ascertained and taken into account
as an important part of the learning plan.

Various instruments are available to accomplish this objective. David Kolb's *Learning Styles Inventory*, for example, was developed especially in reference to experiential learning.

Emphasize the Learner's Role

2.3 An important principle that applies at this point is that the learning process is enhanced when the learner is required to assume significant responsibility for it. The rewarding results are improved self-awareness, enhanced self-confidence and a more effective relationship between what has been learned in the past and what future learning is planned.

Prepare for Field Experience

2.4 Some or all of the steps described above may be undertaken most effectively in an orientation course or seminar. In any case some provision should be made for orientation to the specific learning environment after the learning plan has been developed. Both formative and summative evaluation are enhanced by continuation of a seminar or other regular contact with campus sponsorship during the field learning experience.

Step 3. EVALUATION: Determine the credit equivalency.

Evaluating learning (Does it meet college-creditable standards?) and measuring it (How much has been learned, at what level?) are two vitally important steps in the assessment process. When we are assessing *prior* learning we necessarily must measure first, and then evaluate. For *planned* learning, however, it is useful to evaluate first— i.e., to describe the type and degree of competence that qualifies for a certain amount of credit, before the parties (learner, sponsor, and field personnel) accept a specified commitment. This third step, *evaluation*, will need to be reviewed after completion of the fifth step, *measurement*, to determine whether the measured learning has met the test for the credit. It is the same process that commonly applies to traditional classroom learning: the amount of credit for the course is specified in advance; learning outcomes are (or should be) specified; and the measurement (final exams, term papers, etc.) is applied at the end to determine whether the learning outcomes have met the test for credit.

Decide Who Categorizes and Defines Competences

3.1 Individual institutions decide how standards are to be set. Standards may be defined on the basis of institutional program objectives, the objectives of students, or the requirements of third parties (occupational or educational). It is normally desirable to take all three into account, and institutional policy concerning the standard setting authority should be clear.

Define Criterion and Norm-Referenced Evaluation

3.2 In evaluating any learning plan it should be established as early as practicable what general type of standard will be used as a basis for awarding credit and grades. A sponsored learning program may have established objectives and standards that apply to all participants, or performance standards may be individualized, but, in either event, they are ordinarily stated as learning objectives.

3.21 Whenever possible, it is highly desirable to assess learning in relation to criterion-referenced standards (or, briefly, "criterion standards") of what the individual should be able to do. In the phrase "criterion standards" *criterion* refers to the content or nature of the performance or knowledge indicated and *standards* refers to the depth or level of competence expected.[1]

---

[1] The word "standard" is used differently here than it is elsewhere in this book. The **Ten Standards** which are the primary focus of this work are *process* standards; i.e., measures of the quality of the assessment *process*. "Criterion standards" are *content* standards; i.e., they refer to qualities of the learning *content*.

In defining criterion standards the content or nature of the learning or competence should be stated as clearly as possible through use of appropriate reference and examples.

Useful ways to clarify the content aspects of criterion standards include reference to particular fields and bodies of knowledge, familiar roles or jobs, particular functions the individuals can perform, equipment they can operate, products they are able to produce.

3.22 In defining standards, several levels of competence should be stated as clearly as possible through use of appropriate reference and examples. Ways of clarifying the level or standard expected include using a reference group or a level within a reference group, listing activities commonly associated with particular performance levels, defining whether knowledge is basic or advanced with respect to a specific function, and stating the type of responsibility normally associated with a particular level of competence. When several levels of competence are so defined, different individuals in different programs or institutions might quite rightly receive credit for different levels of competence depending upon the nature of the program.

The term "criterion standards" describes *criterion-referenced* assessment, in contrast to *norm-referenced* assessment. Criterion-referenced assessment judges the level of achievement as compared with predetermined characteristics that are, collectively, labeled as a "criterion." Norm-referenced assessment judges the level of achievement in comparison with that of other persons being assessed. It is sometimes referred to as "grading on the curve." Criterion-referenced assessment measures against a defined level of achievement required for a particular purpose. Norm-referenced assessment measures against the level of achievement of other performers.

Measure Outcomes,
Not Inputs

3.3 Assessment of experiential learning should place emphasis upon criterion-referenced assessment so that individuals are evaluated in terms of expected learning outcomes. In addition, it is frequently desirable to incorporate normative judgments, especially insofar as competence is often conceived in reference to ability to compete at a particular level.

Use Same Standards
For Traditional
and Experiential
Learning

3.4 Standards for crediting experiential learning should be the same as or comparable to standards for crediting learning by more traditional means.

Avoid Duplication

3.5 In recommending credit awards, assessors should take necessary steps to guard against duplication of credit.

Credit Learning,
Not Experience

3.6 The basis for translating learning outcomes into credit hours should be specified. Time spent in an activity should not be a primary consideration in determining credit equivalence. There are other approaches more directly connected with learning outcome: credit hour equivalencies can be established for particular accomplishments; learning outcomes can be matched with those of existing courses. Equivalent academic hours may be estimated for purposes of predicting what learning activities will be necessary, but should not be relied on for direct translation of experience into learning for credit. Formal guidelines are especially desirable to ensure equity in awards.

Use Learning
Contracts

3.7 It is important to clarify criterion standards before the fact so that the student knows what is expected and the learning is guided accordingly. Written learning contracts are a highly desirable means of reaching a clear understanding between student and institution as to the kinds and levels of learning outcomes required for credit.

Integrate Evaluation With Program and Planning

3.8 *Evaluation* (relationship of learning to credit and to grades) and *measurement* (determination of depth and level of learning) should be formative as well as summative.

3.81 A review of prior learning should precede each new learning activity and relate it to the learner's academic objectives.

3.82 The learner should receive feedback during the learning activity to monitor progress toward the intended outcome and to prompt any changes in either objectives or activities that may be indicated.

3.83 Summative feedback should be provided as soon as possible after the completion of the learning activity. It should include explanation of credit awards and implication for degree or other program requirements. The summative evaluation should also serve as the initial step in planning future learning (3.81).

Step 4. DOCUMENTATION: Collect evidence of learning.

Presentation of adequate evidence of learning is an important step in assessment. Such documentation comes in many forms, and different types of documentation serve different functions and have different characteristics. In institutionally sponsored experiential learning programs, documentation often involves a personal verification from a site supervisor plus learning products and/or a detailed record produced by the student.

Develop an   4.1 Institutions should formulate a clear
Institutional Policy policy as to what types of learning require
                        documentation and what function the
                        documentation is intended to serve. It is
                        useful to recognize that documentation
                        may serve several distinguishable func-
                        tions. For example: (a) organizing proper
                        documentation may in itself be a useful
                        learning experience for the student even if
                        it serves no administrative purpose; (b)
                        documentation can be viewed as an accu-
                        mulation of information useful in assess-
                        ment; (c) documentation can be seen largely
                        as a means of consulting third-party
                        expertise; and d) documentation can serve
                        as a useful record for either the student or
                        the institution.

                        4.11 Important functions of documentation
                        are self-assessment and formative evalu-
                        ation of learning progress. (See also 3.7,
                        above.)

Specify Appropriate 4.2 There should be clear institutional
Documentation   specifications as to what types of documen-
                        tation are appropriate for what types of
                        learning.

                        4.21 Students should be provided with
                        descriptions and examples of different
                        types of documentation, the functions they
                        serve, and how they should be solicited and
                        presented. Types of documentation include
                        the following: (a) testimony regarding
                        competence (e.g., evaluative letters or job
                        performance reports); (b) learning products
                        (e.g., essays, work samples, learning logs);
                        (c) performance on examinations, oral or
                        written; (d) demonstrations or simulations.

4.22 Guidelines for documentation should make clear in what ways documentation provided by the student might be used in assessment.

Distinguish Between Experience and Learning

4.3 Care should be taken in discriminating whether particular documentation describes experience, describes learning, or provides evidence of learning. (Evidence of learning may be direct in the form of a detailed report or other student product or indirect in the form of evaluative testimony.)

4.31 Descriptions of a learning activity may or may not, depending upon detail, constitute evidence of learning. Documentation of the fact that a student participated in a learning activity should not in itself be accepted as adequate evidence of learning. Either type of information may well prove useful for direct assessment. In some instances documentation that an individual has participated in an activity may constitute adequate evidence of learning. This can occur when participation is contingent upon having mastered certain competences or qualifications. In this case, the screening or testing associated with the activities serves as a surrogate assessment process. For example, entry into certain civil service jobs requires demonstration of particular competences. Similarly, a certificate or award sometimes provides reasonable assurance of specific learning. (The ACE Guides and the PONSI service are generally accepted examples of a "formula conversion" of experience into evidence of creditable learning.)

4.32 If certificates or similar documentation are taken as evidence of specific competence, periodic checks should be undertaken to ensure that the meaning of the certificate has not changed.

Authenticate the Evidence

4.4 Assessors should take all reasonable and necessary steps to ensure that evidence of learning is accurate and that the student is in fact responsible for work presented. There should be written guidelines as to what constitutes authentic documentation.

4.41 Procedures for obtaining letters to document learning should serve to clarify the nature of the learning and the dependability of the source of evidence.

4.42 The credentials of individuals writing letters in support of student learning should be clear. Individuals writing such letters should know the student and have first-hand knowledge of the experiential learning cited. A documentation letter should state the nature of the author's relationship to the student as well as the author's credentials as an expert judge. (Otherwise, evidence of a conflict of interest or bias may be overlooked.) If appropriate, the letter should be written on official stationery.

4.43 It should be made clear (by either the student or the faculty member, or both) to persons who provide documentation of learning that what is being requested is evidence of the level and depth of learning—not a recommendation for credit or for grading.

Emphasize Quality, Not Quantity	4.5 Care must be exercised to ensure that the quantity and the attractiveness of the presentation of evidence does not influence the award of credit. Credit awards must be based on learning, not experience (**Standard I**), and must be based on accurate measurement of the college-level quality and depth of the learning (*Step 5*, below).

Step 5. MEASUREMENT: Determine the degree and level of competence achieved.

This step in assessment involves determining the extent and character of the knowledge or skill acquired. The principles and procedures that are followed in this part of the process will support the achievement of several of the **Ten Standards**. Perhaps most importantly these principles and procedures are clearly related to **Standard IV**: ensuring that competency judgments are made by qualified experts. There is also a close relationship with **Standard IX**: the vital role of adequate training of assessors. Accuracy of judgment is particularly essential since inconsistency from one judge to another is unfair to students and may discredit the assessment process. Quality assurance depends on both the reliability (5.4) and validity (5.5) of the measurement process.[2]

Fit Assessment Method to Learning Activity	5.1 Assessment of experiential learning should employ measurement methods that fit the character of the learning. Some learning experiences develop competence in a specific well-established subject area, in which case a standard appraisal technique like an objective test may be appropriate and desirable. Much experiential learning, however, is characterized by different learning outcomes for different individuals.

---

[2] A useful reference on measurement is *A Compendium of Assessment Techniques*, written by Joan Knapp and Amiel Sharon and published by CAEL. (See Reference #9 on p. 103.) Stephen Yelon and John Duley are the authors of a booklet specifically on the measurement of *sponsored* experiential learning: *Efficient Evaluation of Individual Performance in Field Placement*. (See Reference # 13 on p. 104.)

In this case, more holistic methods of expert judgment are required to determine the nature and level of individual learning outcomes. These include: product assessment, interviews, oral examinations, simulations, essays, performance assessment, work checklists, etc.

Fit Assessment Method to the Learner

5.2 In measuring an individual's learning, assessors should use techniques that are appropriate to the background and characteristics of the learner. In no event should an extraneous handicap (e.g., speech problem) be allowed to invalidate the assessment.

Utilize Assessment As Learning

5.3 Assessment should be a useful learning experience for the student. Whenever possible the assessment process should be an integral part of the learning process. It is important that assessment goals be reflected in the learning activity, and that learners understand the nature of the assessment process and what function it serves. An appreciation of the purpose of assessment helps to reinforce a sense of the individual's responsibility for her or his own learning and a sense of mutual accountability with the faculty. Improved self-awareness and better understanding of the techniques of self-assessment are important learning outcomes of assessment and can serve the student in later life. Thus, assessment should be perceived partly as instruction and partly as evaluation and measurement of learning. Both the formative and summative stages of evaluative measurement offer excellent opportunities to develop the skills of self-directed learning.

Ensure Reliability

5.4 Institutions should strive to see that assessment is as reliable (consistent) as possible in order to ensure fairness to students.

5.41 To improve consistency in assessment judgments, more than one sample of learning should be examined whenever possible and more than one assessor should be used unless other evidence indicates that one is sufficient. Research indicates that judgments of different assessors can vary considerably and systematically if they have had limited experience or if assessment guidelines are not clear. Serious inequity to students can result. It is advisable for institutions to use multiple assessors until experience indicates that learning can be judged with acceptable consistency by assessors working independently.

5.42 Assessors should strive to avoid any form of bias, discrimination, or unconscious error in judging student performance or work. Ratings that are either too favorable or too severe may result from a number of common errors including the following:

• the tendency to avoid the extremes of the scale and to rate at average;

• allowing an outstanding, or inferior, trait or aspect of performance to influence the rating of other factors (halo effect);

• judging according to a personal stereotype or strongly held (but not as strongly relevant) attitude;

• the tendency to prejudge individuals by an initial impression rather than on the basis of observed performance;

• the tendency to rate a student more favorably if the student is similar to the rater in background, attitudes, or ethnic group;

• the tendency to rate a student lower than average when the assessment immediately follows that of an outstanding student, or to give a higher than average rating in an assessment immediately following that of a very poor student (contrast effect).

Ensure Validity

5.5 It is essential to ensure that assessment is valid, i.e. that assessors measure what is intended. Validity of assessment will be improved if there are institutional guidelines as to what constitutes college-level learning, what learning is creditable to particular degrees, what the established objectives of experiential learning programs are, and what specific learning goals students may have contracted for. It is important for institutions not only to describe learning that is creditable under various circumstances, but to provide assessors (and students, where possible) with illustrations—examples of creditable learning and also examples of learning that is not creditable and the reasons why. Similarly, assessment procedures that involve ratings of products or performance should include examples of learning at different levels of competence clearly designated.

5.51 Whenever possible, it is highly desirable to assess learning by direct comparison with learning objectives or criterion standards previously stated in clear language. (This principle is not meant to preclude recognition of unexpected learning outcomes.)

5.52 Whenever appropriate, assessors should seek different forms of evidence of learning and use more than one type of assessment in order to reach a valid judgment. If, for example, a student seeks credit for an unusual set of accomplishments or a variety of specialized work competences, it may be necessary to obtain (a) detailed information concerning the character of the achievement and testimony as to the accuracy of the claim, and (b) an expert assessment from another source as to the depth of such learning.

5.53 Even though assessors may agree in assessing a particular type of learning, special caution is suggested if they do not agree on how such learning is related to the curriculum. CAEL research has revealed such results in some instances of assessing occupational competences and interpersonal skills. The danger in such circumstances is that the assessment is invalid because the assessors are agreeing on some superficial aspect of performance without a clear understanding of its educational value or meaning.

Train the Assessors   5.6 An essential safeguard for quality assurance is provision for professional development of all personnel involved in the measurement of learning (**Standard IX**).

5.61 Assessment should be carefully planned. Detailed written procedures, instructions, and background material should be available to faculty concerning any assessment procedure routinely used.

5.62 Specialized assessment techniques, such as role playing or simulation, should not be promoted for use unless there are assessors readily available who are sufficiently familiar with such methods to use them competently.

5.63 Reasonably standard conditions and arrangements for assessment should be maintained in accord with institutional guidelines unless the nature of the assessment problem suggests otherwise, in which case deviations in procedures should be clarified and agreed to beforehand. While it is important to fit the assessment to the learning and to the student, assessors should be encouraged to adhere to guidelines that have been carefully drawn to ensure fair assessment. Furthermore, certain arrangements (location and length of an assessment session, the people involved, etc.) may appear especially important to students, and unexplained deviations could be cause for concern and a poor assessment.

State Results Objectively

5.7 Insofar as possible, the results of individual assessment should be objectively stated. Even though the assessment process may emphasize a subjective, holistic judgment, the outcome of the assessment should be as explicit as possible in identifying what specific learning outcomes were involved, what levels of competence were reached, and what standards were employed. Objectivity not only fosters accurate assessment and minimizes misinterpretation, it also facilitates quality control of the assessment process itself by making it possible to compare assessments and to determine how they were reached.

Encourage Supervised Self-assessment

5.8 Self-assessment is not a sufficient basis upon which to grant credit. It can, however, be a powerful aid to learning. To the extent that an institution relies upon self-assessment in instruction, special care must be taken to assure that it does not prejudice the efforts of more objective assessors, or substitute for work which they should perform. In self-assessment, the same special care as in assessment by others should be taken to define learning objectives clearly and to assemble evidence that objectives have been achieved. A few institutions place considerable stress upon self-assessment for pedagogical reasons and are willing to place considerable weight upon the student's judgment as to whether learning objectives have been met. When self-assessment is properly used, it is supplemented with appropriate steps to educate the student on how to assume responsibility and how to present evidence of learning so that it can be verified by the appropriate faculty member before credit is awarded or grades assigned by the faculty.

5.81 Learner participation in both the design and administration of the assessment process is desirable as a means of enhancing personal development, particularly the sharpening of self-directed learning skills. The opportunity for learner participation in the process is maximized in

sponsored learning programs where the
learning objectives are specified in advance.

Step 6: TRANSCRIPTION: Prepare a useful record of results.

Since experiential learning often emphasizes application of knowledge and the development of competence rather than a mastery of traditional theoretical and factual subject matter, usual course labels often do not serve well in describing such learning. The experiential learning often covers parts of two or more catalog courses. Given the particular objective of the learning and the pattern of learning already completed or planned, a precise convergence with catalog courses may not be necessary. However, the transcript credential is the only means many third parties have for knowing about the learning and how it contributes to a degree or other program objective. For these reasons, accurate description and recording of learning outcomes is an important and integral part of the assessment process.

For the awarding institution the maintenance of quality should already have been assured before reaching the transcribing process. For transfer institutions and other third parties the transcript should contain the evidence needed to substantiate satisfaction of **Standard I** (credit for learning, not experience), **Standard III** (balance of theoretical and applied learning), **Standard V** (application to degree or other certification), and **Standard VI** (avoiding duplication). It is, however, not sufficient merely to indicate that credit was earned in an *experiential* learning program. Such a practice reflects and extends the error of confusing *inputs* (e.g., experiential learning activities) with learning *outcomes* (i.e., particular knowledge or skill competence).

Communicate with Third Parties	6.1 Transcripts should communicate effectively with third parties, especially employers and admission officers considering applications for work or further study.
	6.11 Institutions developing narrative transcripts should appoint user review panels to react to the proposed content and format. Appropriate reviewers include students, representatives of public and private employers, and graduate and professional admissions personnel.

6.12 In designing transcripts, it is desirable to balance carefully (a) the need for clear description of the important unique aspects of the individual student's learning, and (b) the necessity to present succinct credentials that are likely to be given adequate attention by third parties.

Record Learning Appropriately

6.2 Credit or other recognition of learning should be recorded on the student's transcript in a manner appropriate to the learning and to the function of the transcript as an accurate and comprehensive record of the student's learning.

6.21 When learning is highly individualized, entering credit under arbitrary course labels is often not descriptive and may give inaccurate impressions. Some alternative is desirable: narrative descriptions, statement of outcomes using commonly accepted terms within the relevant disciplines, etc.

6.22 Course labels or abbreviated descriptions of learning may be adequate for transcripts when they refer to specific syllabi or detailed competence statements. For external use in such cases, however, further descriptive information necessary for interpretation should be part of the transcript or should be readily available.

6.23 Regardless of the exact form of the credential, it is important that institutions strive to describe through the transcript what the student knows or can do, not simply verify time served.

Describe Content and Level

6.3 There are two essential elements of a good transcript. It must describe (a) the

content of learning (i.e., what competence
or knowledge was involved) and (b) the
level of learning (i.e., what scope or depth
was achieved). Both ends are served well if
content and levels of competence are clearly
differentiated in the statement of learning
objectives.

6.31 When appropriate, transcripts should
identify the auspices under which learning
is acquired, especially when the conditions
of learning and assessment are different
from what may be assumed by a third
party. For example, one might differentiate
and identify independent study, field experience learning, internships, and cooperative education.[3]

6.32 Transcripts should include additional
information as may be necessary to make
clear the nature of the learning represented.
Other information that may be relevant to
particular types of learning includes: dates
when learning took place so that third
parties might better judge whether learning
is still current; details such as location,
supervision, or duration, which may bear
upon quality of learning; an indication of
how the learning was documented and assessed and what standards were employed.

---

[3] When the credits that are awarded are expressed in terms of explicitly stated learning
outcomes, this procedure (6.31) should not be necessary. *Ideally* all transcripts would
describe the level and content of skills and knowledge acquired (i.e., the learning
outcomes). The sources of the learning would be irrelevant. *Realistically,* however,
many consumers of transcript information still base important decisions on their
perceptions of the *source* of learning, rather than exclusively on its level and content.
Until this practice disappears it would be unfair to learners if the source of learning
were not specified on the transcript.

Chapter Four
Principles and Procedures for Assessing Prior Experiential Learning[1]

In the Prologue to this description of principles and procedures (see p. 19, above) we have described the reason why the assessment of prior experiential learning requires a different sequence of steps than those used in more traditional assessments. In Table Two we have listed six Steps for assessing prior experiential learning and related them to the **standards** they serve.

Step 1 is the *identification* of potentially creditable prior learning. The primary responsibility for completing this step rests with the learner. However, a successful outcome is significantly enhanced when the process is undertaken as part of a formal portfolio course. Within a course, or at the very least a strong advising program, it is much easier to ascertain the requirements of **Standards I** and **II**. These core requirements (credit is granted only for college-level learning) must be the primary guidelines for identifying potentially creditable prior experiential learning.

In *Step 2* the learner along with a faculty adviser must relate the claimed learning to the requirements of the relevant academic program (**Standard V**). This may also be an important checkpoint concerning the learner's personal and career goals. When prior learning in support of these goals has already taken place there may be

---

[1] The term "prior experiential learning" excludes certain kinds of learning, both traditional and experiential, that have already been evaluated and transcribed. In this chapter we address that area of potentially college-creditable learning that has been acquired through work or other experience, or that has been acquired through more traditional but not college-sponsored means, such as workshops and training courses in business, industry, or military settings.

Table Two:
The Assessment of Prior Experiential Learning

STEPS	DIVISION OF RESPONSIBILITY	RELEVANT STANDARDS
1. IDENTIFICATION: Review experience to identify potentially creditable learning.	Primary responsibility rests with the faculty, but ideally assisted by portfolio course.	Standards I and II. (Credit is for learning, not for experience, and it must be college-level.)
2. ARTICULATION: Relate proposed credit to academic, personal, and professional goals.	Joint responsibility of learner and faculty.	Standard V. (Learning must be relevant to academic program and goals.)
3. DOCUMENTATION: Prepare evidence to support claim for credit.	Primary responsibility rests with the learner, but ideally is assisted by a portfolio course.	Standards I, II, and III. (Credit is granted only for college-level learning with appropriate balance of theory and practice.)
4. MEASUREMENT: Determine the degree and level of competence achieved.	Faculty.	Standards I, II, and III.
5. EVALUATION: Determine the credit equivalency.	Faculty.	Standard IV. (Credit awards must be made by faculty.)
6. TRANSCRIPTION: Prepare a useful record of results.	Administration with advice of appropriate faculty.	Standard VI. (Avoid duplication.)

advantages, beyond meeting the requirements of the academic program, to having the learning officially recognized and recorded.

In *Step 3, documentation,* the learner has the primary responsibility for preparing the evidence that college-creditable learning has taken place (**Standards I** and **II**) and that it contributes to an appropriate balance of theory and practical application (**Standard III**). Again there is a significant advantage in approaching this step as part of a formally scheduled portfolio course.

Steps 4 and *5,* measuring the learning and determining credit awards, are the heart of the assessment process. These are faculty responsibilities (**Standard IV**) and the faculty must ensure that **Standards I, II, III** and **V** have been met. In determining the amount of credit the faculty needs to look beyond the confirmation (or denial) of the learning claimed in *Step 1.* On the one hand, the assessment process may have identified additional creditable learning. On the other hand, some or all of the claimed learning may be creditable only after the completion of additional coursework or independent study. *Step 5* is also an important opportunity to review the learner's academic, personal and career goals, taking advantage of new insights flowing from the results of the assessment.

Step 6, transcribing the results, is usually an administrative function. However, in the case of prior learning outcomes it is particularly important for the faculty member to provide complete information about the results. Meeting the requirements of **Standard VI** (avoid duplication) may depend on judgments which can only be made by the faculty member.

The remainder of this chapter is devoted to a more detailed discussion of the principles and procedures that support the **Ten Standards** of quality assurance. These principles and procedures are also summarized in the form of a checklist in Appendix B.

Step 1: IDENTIFICATION: Review experience to identify potentially creditable learning.

This is a critical stage in the assessment of prior experiential learning because of the obvious need to know as clearly as possible what competence or knowledge there is to be assessed. It is typically a very difficult but personally valuable step for students seeking credit for learning acquired prior to enrollment. For the most part, prior experiential learning lacks the advantage of pre-planned learning objectives, learning activities, and assessment methods. Thus the first important step in assessment is to discover and to describe college-level learning that may have resulted from learning activities that did not include the assessment as part of the process.

Define "College Level"

1.1 Only college-level learning should be credited by colleges and universities (**Standard I**). The institution should provide clear guidelines (including principles and examples) as to what it considers to be college-level (**Standard VII**). Three characteristics are often considered important: (a) that the learning imply a conceptual as well as a practical grasp of the knowledge or competence acquired (**Standard III**); (b) that the learning be applicable outside the specific context in which it was acquired; and (c) that the learning fall within the domain usually considered appropriate for postsecondary credit as opposed to secondary or continuing education for non-credit purposes. The essential point is that the guidelines should faithfully reflect institutional policy regarding the domain of college-level learning.

1.11 To respond effectively to the multiple sources and circumstances in which creditable learning can occur, it is necessary to identify a number of options for determining the college level of prior learning. Possible bases for justification include the following:

• relating learning to subject areas traditionally taught in colleges;

• showing that what was learned is at a level of achievement equal to what is normal in colleges;

• comparing specific learning to that acquired in college-level work;

• relating learning to a personal goal that requires college-level learning;

• identifying learning as that acquired after high school and expected for professional acceptance.

Describe Learning Experiences

1.2 As an aid to recalling and identifying learning, it is often useful for students first to describe the experiences in which the learning occurred. In the case of prior learning, various techniques may be helpful in recalling and recording pertinent experiences, e.g., through use of a time-line, resume, work description, or autobiography. CAEL has focused upon portfolio-assisted assessment as a means of organizing the evidence and petitioning for prior learning credit. "Portfolio" is here a generic term that refers both to a product and to a process of assembling pertinent information; it can be defined and used in a variety of ways. However, it must be emphasized that assessors should be assessing the *learning*, not the portfolio.[2]

Differentiate Between Learning and Experience

1.3 Students should be required to differentiate between learning and experience. Learning outcomes should be expressed in terms appropriate to the institution's curriculum and assessment procedures.

Specify Outcomes

1.4 Learning outcomes should be identified with enough specificity that they can be

---

[2] See Malpractice #4, Chapter Six, p. 98.

readily communicated and assessed. Terms that describe broad learning goals like "communication," "analysis," or "management" are frequently useful in classifying learning outcomes, but may not be helpful in making clear what learning was accomplished. To say that a person has learned to communicate may mean many different things at different levels of competence. More specific descriptions of learning are necessary if faculty and student are to know clearly what can be credited and to recognize when learning has in fact taken place. Ideally, descriptions of learning should also clarify what the student should be competent to do as a result of the learning.

1.41 Clarity and specificity in describing learning outcomes should not be achieved by relegating learning objectives to trivial skills.

Consider the Recency of Learning

1.5 For those forms of prior learning most commonly assessed, there should be a stated policy with respect to the recency or currency of learning that is expected if credit is to be awarded. Insofar as possible, such policies should avoid inconsistencies with standard practices in transcript evaluation of students transferring or reentering college.

Use Assessment to Reinforce Learning

1.6 Identification of learning should proceed in a manner that reinforces what has been learned, fosters improved self-awareness, enhances self-confidence, and emphasizes the importance of students' assuming responsibility for their own learning.

Facilitate Reentry and Future Learning

1.7 It is highly desirable to provide some specific mechanisms that will not only help the student to identify prior learning but will also facilitate reentry into higher education. Many students petitioning for credit for prior learning will have been absent from formal education for some time and may be unsure of themselves and how to proceed. Furthermore, the process of developing a portfolio of prior learning is difficult for many students. With proper support, however, it frequently proves to be an extremely valuable learning experience. Consequently, it is particularly important to provide some formal mechanism for assisting students. Possibilities include counseling, mentoring, workshops, educational planning courses, and self-instructional materials.

1.71 Students should be provided with explanatory materials concerning assessment of prior learning, including examples of portfolio materials.

1.72 A formal course is very desirable for orienting students to assessment of prior learning. It serves, in the first place, as *instruction* (i.e., it is planned learning) for one of the most important and basic learning objectives: learning how to learn. It can be a vital link between the assessment of prior learning and the improvement of future planned learning. A credit-bearing course has many other advantages. It signals serious intent and acknowledges that acquiring expertise in educational planning and assessment is important in the institution's system of values. A course offers a good means for magnifying the

educational value of assessment. It also
provides a vehicle for monitoring progress
and providing assistance as needed. Furthermore, a formal course offers the added
advantage of providing a routine means of
recognizing the faculty time as a legitimate
instructional cost.

**Step 2: ARTICULATION: Relate proposed credit to academic, per-
sonal, and professional goals.**

The fact that learning is determined to be college level is not
ordinarily a sufficient basis for granting college credit. In most instances the validity of a learning experience for credit purposes
depends upon a demonstrated relationship to a defined degree or
other program objective. The principles and procedures discussed in
this section are supportive of quality assurance with respect to **Standard V** (learning must be appropriate to academic context).

Determine What Is Creditable	2.1 There should be an institutional rationale for crediting particular types of learning or competences to particular degree programs, especially if there is some difference of opinion among postsecondary institutions regarding credibility.
Balance Theory and Applied Learning	2.2 There should be an institutional rationale concerning the most appropriate mix of experiential and theoretic learning, including how and when the two should be included in the student's educational plan.
Relate to Program Objectives	2.3 Institutions should require individuals petitioning for credit to specify satisfactorily how prior experiential learning contributes to the individual's degree or other program objectives.
	2.31 In identifying and articulating learning that is related to educational goals, the student should look both backward and

forward—backward to integrate past
learning and to identify important gaps,
and forward to plan continued learning
that builds effectively on the foundation of
the prior learning assessment.

Step 3. DOCUMENTATION: Prepare evidence to support claim for credit.

Documentation of prior learning comes in many forms, including certificates, letters, awards, and such direct evidence as work samples or other learning products. Presentation of adequate evidence of learning is a vital step in the assessment process and a prerequisite for quality assurance in achieving **Standards I, II** and **III** (credit only for college-level learning that has an appropriate balance of theoretical and applied knowledge and skills).

Develop an Institutional Policy	3.1 Institutions should formulate a clear policy as to what types of learning require documentation and what function such documentation is intended to serve.
	3.11 In the case of prior learning, reliance on documentation depends upon the extent to which the institution intends to assess learning directly. Some institutions lay special stress on accumulating documentation while others prefer to assess directly. It is useful to recognize that documentation may serve several mutually exclusive functions. For example: (a) organizing proper documentation may in itself be a useful learning experience for the student even if it serves no administrative purpose; (b) documentation can be viewed as an accumulation of descriptive information useful in assessment; (c) documentation can be seen largely as a means of consulting third-party expertise; and (d) documentation can serve as a record for both the student and the institution.

Specify Appropriate Documentation

3.2 There should be clear institutional specifications as to what types of documentation are appropriate for what types of learning.[3]

3.21 Students should be provided with descriptions and examples of different types of documentation, the functions they serve, and how they should be solicited and presented. Types of documentation include the following: (a) verification of accomplishment (e.g., a prize or musical program); (b) testimony regarding competence (e.g., evaluative letters or job performance reports); (c) learning products (e.g., learning logs, essays, work samples, or art objects); (d) certification (e.g., licenses or rank attained); (e) other direct evidence (e.g., publications or test scores); (f) descriptions (e.g., syllabi, membership requirements, or job descriptions).

3.22 Guidelines for documentation should make clear in what ways documentation might be used in assessment.

Distinguish Types of Evidence

3.3 Care should be taken in discriminating whether particular documentation describes experience, describes learning, or provides evidence of learning. Evidence of learning may be direct in the form of a detailed report or other student product or indirect in the form of evaluative testimony.

3.31 Descriptions of a learning activity may or may not, depending upon detail, constitute evidence of learning. Documentation of

---

[3] An appropriate tool for this purpose is Susan Simosko's book, *Earn College Credit for What You Know.* (See Reference #11 on p. 104.)

the fact that a student participated in a learning activity should not in itself be considered to constitute adequate evidence of learning. Either type of information may well prove useful for direct assessment. In some instances documentation that an individual has participated in an activity may constitute adequate evidence of learning. This can occur when participation is contingent upon having mastered certain competences. In this case, the screening or testing associated with the activities serves as a surrogate assessment process. For example, entry into certain civil service jobs requires demonstration of particular competences. Similarly, a certificate or award sometimes provides reasonable assurance of specific learning.

3.32 If certificates or similar documentation are taken as evidence of specific competence, periodic checks should be undertaken to ensure that the meaning of the certificate has not changed.

Authenticate Evidence

3.4 Assessors should take all reasonable steps to ensure that evidence of learning is accurate and that the student is in fact responsible for work presented. There should be written guidelines as to what constitutes authentic documentation.

3.41 Procedures for obtaining letters to document learning should serve to clarify the nature of the learning and the dependability of the source of evidence.

3.42 The credentials of individuals writing letters in support of student learning should be clear. Individuals writing such letters should know the student and have first-hand knowledge of the experiential learning cited. A documentation letter should state the nature of the author's relationship to the student as well as the author's credentials as an expert judge. If appropriate, the letter should be written on official stationery.

3.43 In evaluating performance, authors of documenting letters should be asked to give an accurate indication of level of competence in relation to a criterion standard and, if possible, to compare the student's performance with that of individuals in a known reference group. An indication of personal development should be included if appropriate. Documenting letters should not be perceived merely as letters of recommendation or commendation. The content of documenting letters should include, but not be limited to, a description of the duties, responsibilities, and tasks involved in the experiential learning under consideration.

Emphasize Quality, 3.5 Excessive documentation, attractively
Not Quantity presented, should not compensate for poor performance in assessment or questionable relevance of learning to the degree objective.

Step 4. MEASUREMENT: Determine the degree and level of competence achieved.

This step in assessment involves determining the extent and character of the knowledge or skill acquired. The principles and procedures that are followed in this part of the process will support the achievement of several of the **Ten Standards**. Perhaps most importantly these principles and procedures are clearly related to **Standard IV**: ensuring that competency judgments are made by qualified experts. There is also a close relationship with **Standard IX**: the role of adequate training of assessors. Accuracy of judgment is particularly essential since inconsistency from one judge to another is unfair to students and may discredit the assessment process. Quality assurance depends on both the reliability (4.4) and validity (4.5) of the measurement process.[4]

Fit Assessment Method to Learning Activity	4.1 Assessment of experiential learning should employ measurement methods that fit the character of the learning. Some learning experiences develop competence in a specific well-established subject area, in which case a standard appraisal technique like an objective test may be appropriate and desirable. Much experiential learning, however, is characterized by different learning outcomes for different individuals. In this case, more holistic methods of expert judgment are required to determine the nature and level of individual learning outcomes. These include product assessment, interviews, oral examinations, simulations, essays, performance assessment, etc.
Fit Assessment Method to the Learner	4.2 In measuring an individual's learning, assessors should use techniques that are appropriate to the background and characteristics of the learner. In no event should an extraneous handicap (e.g., speech problem or severe shyness) be allowed to invalidate the assessment.
Utilize Assessment As Learning	4.3 Assessment should be, in itself, a useful learning experience for the student. Whenever possible the assessment process should

---

[4] A useful reference on measurement is *A Compendium of Assessment Techniques*, written by Joan Knapp and Amiel Sharon and published by CAEL. (See References # 9 on p. 103.)

be an integral part of the learning process. It is important that learners understand the nature of the assessment process and what function it serves. An appreciation of the purpose of assessment helps to reinforce a sense of the individual's responsibility for her or his own learning and a sense of mutual accountability with the faculty. Improved self-awareness and better understanding of the techniques of self-assessment are important learning outcomes of assessment and can serve the student in later life. Thus assessment should be perceived partly as the measurement and evaluation of learning and partly as instruction—particularly instruction in the important process of "learning how to learn."

Ensure Reliability   4.4 Institutions should strive to see that assessment is as reliable (consistent) as possible in order to ensure fairness to students.

4.41 To improve consistency in assessment judgments, more than one sample of learning should be examined whenever possible and more than one assessor should be used unless evidence indicates that one is sufficient. Research indicates that judgments of different assessors can vary considerably and systematically if they have had limited experience or if assessment guidelines are not clear. Serious inequity to students can result. It is advisable, therefore, for institutions to use multiple assessors until experience indicates that learning can be judged with acceptable consistency (i.e., by different assessors working independently).

4.42 Assessors should strive to avoid any form of bias, discrimination, or unconscious error in judging student performance or work. The following are common types of errors:

• the tendency to rate too liberally or too severely;

• the tendency to avoid the extremes of the scale and to rate at the average;

• allowing an outstanding or inferior trait or aspect of performance to influence the rating of other factors (halo effect);

• judging the candidate according to a personal stereotype or strongly-held attitude;

• the tendency to prejudge by an initial impression rather than on the basis of observed performance;

• the tendency to rate a student more favorably if the student is similar to the rater in background, attitudes, or ethnic group;

• the tendency to rate a student lower than average when the assessment immediately follows that of an outstanding student, or to give a higher than average rating in an assessment immediately following that of a very poor student (contrast effect).

Ensure Validity

4.5 It is essential to ensure that assessment is valid, i.e., that assessors measure what is intended. Validity of assessment will be improved if there are institutional guidelines as to what constitutes college-level learning, what learning is creditable to particular degrees, and what the established objectives of experiential learning programs are. It is important for institutions not only to describe learning that is creditable under various circumstances, but to provide assessors (and students, where possible) with illustrations—examples of creditable learning and also examples of learning not creditable and the reasons why. Similarly, assessment procedures that involve ratings of products or performance should include examples of learning at different levels of competence clearly designated.

4.51 Whenever possible, it is highly desirable to assess learning by direct comparison with learning objectives or criterion standards stated in clear language so that it is possible to decide whether the learning has or has not been acquired. Institutions where course requirements are stated in competency-based terms will find it easier to ensure validity than will institutions whose course requirements are characterized by input rather than outcome statements.

4.52 Whenever appropriate, assessors should seek different forms of evidence of learning and use more than one type of assessment in order to reach a valid judgment. If, for example, a student seeks credit for an unusual set of accomplishments or a variety of specialized work competences, it may be necessary to obtain (a) detailed information concerning the character of the achievement and testimony as to the accuracy of the claim, and (b) an expert assessment from another source as to the depth of such learning and an appropriate basis for determining credit equivalence.

4.53 Even though assessors may agree in assessing a particular type of learning, special caution is suggested if they do not agree on how such learning is related to the curriculum. CAEL research revealed such results in some instances of assessing occupational competences and interpersonal skills. The danger in such circumstances is that the assessment is invalid because the assessors are agreeing on some superficial aspect of performance without a clear understanding of its educational meaning or value.

Plan the Process and Train the Assessors

4.6 Proper safeguards should be employed to ensure that assessment is well-designed and competently administered by appropriately trained assessors.

4.61 All assessment should be carefully planned. Detailed written procedures, instructions, and background material should be available to faculty concerning any assessment procedure routinely used.

4.62 Due to its flexibility in dealing with highly individual learning, the assessment interview is a common method of assessing experiential learning. If the interview is to support reliable and valid assessment, it is particularly important that it be carefully planned and carried out.

4.63 Specialized assessment techniques such as role-playing or simulation should not be promoted for use unless there are

assessors readily available who are sufficiently familiar with such methods to use
them with confidence.

4.64 Reasonably standard conditions and
arrangments for assessment should be
maintained in accord with institutional
guidelines unless the nature of the assessment problem suggests otherwise, in which
case deviations in procedures should be
clarified and agreed to beforehand.

While it is imperative to fit the assessment
to the learning and to the student, assessors
should be encouraged to follow guidelines
that have been carefully drawn to ensure
fair assessment. Certain arrangements
(location and length of an assessment
session, the people involved, etc.) may
appear especially important to students,
and unexplained deviation could be cause
for concern and a poor assessment.

**State Results
Objectively**

4.7 Insofar as possible, the results of individual assessment should be objectively
stated. Even though the assessment process
may emphasize a subjective, holistic
judgment, the assessment should be as
explicit as possible in identifying what
specific learning outcomes were involved,
what levels of competence were reached,
and what standards were employed.
Objectivity not only fosters accurate assessment and minimizes misinterpretation, it
also facilitates quality control of the assessment process itself by making it possible to
compare assessments and to determine
how they were reached.

Encourage Supervised Self-assessment	4.8 Self-assessment is often very desirable as a means of enhancing personal development and awareness of the implications of acquired skills. It is also an important element in learning about the learning process.

4.81 Self-assessment is not a sufficient basis upon which to grant credit. To the extent that an institution relies, in some degree, upon self-assessment, special care must be taken to define learning outcomes clearly and to assemble evidence that they have been achieved. A few institutions place considerable stress upon self-assessment for pedagogical reasons and are willing to place considerable weight on the student's judgment as to whether learning objectives have been met. When self-assessment is properly used, it is supervised with appropriate steps to educate the student on how to assume responsibility for her or his own education and how to present evidence of learning so that it may be verified by the appropriate faculty member before credit is awarded.

Step 5. EVALUATION: Determine the credit equivalency.

Unlike the assessment of sponsored learning, prior learning assessment requires that *measurement* (How much has been learned, and at what level of competence?—*Step 4*, above) must be completed before *evaluation* (Does the learning meet college-creditable standards and, if so, how much credit should be awarded?). Since this is the crucial and final step before any credit should be awarded for prior learning, it is not surprising that it is directly related to nearly all of the **Ten Standards** (as indicated by bold face references at appropriate points in the text).

**Determine the
Criteria for
Evaluation**

5.1 In evaluating any petition for credit, it should be established before the assessment process begins what criteria will be applied in determining the award of credit. In the case of prior learning, the criteria for awarding credit or other recognition may, depending upon the nature of the learning and the institution, be based upon existing competence statements, corresponding course content, degree requirements, or other means of judging the relevance and quality of learning. It is essential to assess learning with reference to what the individual should be able to do. Both the content or nature of the performance or knowledge indicated and the depth or level of competence expected are vital. Together these qualities must add up to college-level learning (**Standard II**).

5.11 The content or nature of the learning or competence should be stated as clearly as possible through the use of appropriate references and examples. Useful ways to clarify the content include reference to particular fields and bodies of knowledge, familiar roles or jobs, particular functions individuals can perform, equipment they can operate, products they are able to complete.

5.12 Several levels of competence should be stated as clearly as possible through use of appropriate reference or examples. Ways of clarifying the level expected include using a reference group, listing activities commonly associated with particular performance levels, defining whether knowledge is basic or advanced with respect to a specific function, and stating the type of responsibility normally associated with a particular level of competence. When several levels of competence are so defined, different individuals in different programs or institutions might quite rightly receive credit for different levels of competence depending upon the nature of the program.

Decide Who Interprets and Applies the Criteria

5.2 Guidelines should include both rationale and procedure regarding the choice of assessors who award credit for experiential learning. In actual practice there are many different arrangements whereby appropriate individuals are chosen to evaluate and make credit recommendations—individual faculty in departments, special assessors, departmental or campus-wide committees, etc. The most important point is that the process must employ expertise both in subject matter content and in evaluation (**Standard IX**).

Ensure Equity in Evaluation and Credit Awards

5.3 All criteria for awarding credit should be rigorous and reasonable in relation to the goals and character of the institution and the nature of its students.

5.31 Criteria for awarding credit for experiential learning should be the same as or comparable to standards for crediting other more traditional forms of learning. Neither should be more or less difficult to attain.

5.32 Evaluation should be in terms of learning outcomes. In addition, it is frequently desirable to incorporate normative judgments, especially insofar as competence is often conceived in reference to ability to compete at a particular level.[5]

---

[5] See footnote #1 (Step 3.21) in Chapter Three, p. 30.

Consider Alternative Types of Recognition

5.4 Institutions should consider granting advanced standing or waivers of some requirements when the award of credit is not justified although the learning constitutes adequate preparation to undertake studies for which some prerequisites are normally expected.

5.41 In recommending credit awards, evaluators should take necessary steps to guard against duplication of credit (**Standard VI**).

Develop and Publish Credit Policies

5.5 Policies and procedures for granting credit for experiential learning should be clearly specified in written guidelines available to students and faculty (**Standard V**).

5.51 The basis for translating learning outcomes into credit hours should be specified. Time spent in an activity should not be the primary consideration in determining credit equivalence (**Standard I**). There are various approaches which provide more nearly direct evaluation of the learning outcome: credit hour equivalencies can be established for particular accomplishments; learning outcomes can be matched with existing courses; equivalent academic hours required to achieve the learning can be estimated. Formal guidelines are especially desirable in order to ensure equity in awards.

Provide for Review and Appeal

5.6 There should be provision for routine review of credit awards whenever it is felt that a "second opinion" is needed, and there should be an established procedure,

of which students are advised, whereby
credit awards can be appealed if there
appears to be due cause.

5.61 The regular review of individual credit
awards should be a part of an established,
more comprehensive process of periodic
review of the entire prior learning credit
process (**Standard X**).

Provide Useful
Feedback

5.7 As soon as possible after the evaluation,
students should receive feedback on the
results, and such feedback should include
explanations for credit awards that deviate
from amount petitioned or expected.

5.71 All credit awards should be based
upon a written evaluation that notes and
explains any departure from established
policy or procedure.

5.72 In providing feedback to the student
concerning evaluation and credits awarded
(or not awarded), it is important to advise
the student regarding implications for
degree requirements, including an appropriate balance of theory and applied
learning (**Standard III**).

5.73 Appropriate mechanisms should be
developed to assist the student in integrat-
ing the results of prior learning assessment
and evaluation into his or her program of
future work. Prior learning assessment
should be recognized as the foundation for
the planning of sponsored learning and not
solely as a means of acquiring credit.

Step 6. TRANSCRIPTION: Prepare a useful record of results.

Since experiential learning often emphasizes application of knowledge and the development of competence rather than a mastery of traditional subject matter, usual course labels often do not serve well in describing such learning. The experiential learning often covers parts of two or more catalog courses. Given the particular objective of the learning and the pattern of learning already completed or planned, the precise convergence with catalog courses may not be necessary. However, the transcript credential is the only means many third parties have for knowing about the learning and how it contributes to a degree or other progam objective. For these reasons, accurate description and recording of learning outcomes is an important and integral part of the assessment process.

For the awarding institution the maintenance of quality should already have been assured before reaching the transcribing process. For transfer institutions and other third parties the transcript should contain the evidence needed to substantiate satisfaction of **Standard I** (credit for learning, not experience), **Standard III** (balance of theoretical and applied learning), **Standard V** (application to degree or other certification), and **Standard VI** (avoidance of duplication). It is, however, not sufficient merely to indicate that credit was earned in an *experiential* learning program. Such a practice reflects and extends the error of confusing *inputs* (e.g., experiential learning activities) with learning *outcomes* (i.e., particular knowledge or skill competence).

Comunicate with Third Parties	6.1 Transcripts should communicate effectively with third parties, especially employers and admission officers considering application for work or further study.
	6.11 Institutions developing narrative transcripts should appoint user review panels to react to the proposed content and format. Appropriate reviewers include students, representatives of public and private employers, and graduate and professional admissions personnel.
	6.12 In designing transcripts, it is desirable

to balance carefully (a) the need for clear description of the important unique aspects of the individual student's learning, and (b) the necessity to present succinct credentials that are likely to be given adequate attention by third parties.

Record Learning Appropriately

6.2 Credit or other recognition of learning should be recorded on the student's transcript in a manner appropriate to the learning and to the function of the transcript as an accurate and comprehensive record of the student's learning.

6.21 When learning is highly individualized, entering credit under arbitrary course labels is often not descriptive and may give inaccurate impressions. Some alternative is desirable: narrative descriptions, statements of outcomes, etc.

6.22 Course labels or abbreviated descriptions of learning may be adequate for transcripts when they refer to specific syllabi or detailed competence statements. In such cases, descriptive information necessary for interpretation should be part of the transcript or should be readily available.

6.23 Regardless of the exact form of the credential, it is important that institutions strive to describe through the transcript what the student knows or can do, not simply to verify time served.

Describe Content and Level

6.3 There are two essential elements of a good transcript: (a) the content of learning; i.e., what competence or knowledge was involved; and (b) the level of learning; i.e., what scope or depth was achieved.

6.31 When appropriate, transcripts should
identify the auspices under which learning
is acquired, especially when the conditions
of learning and assessment are different
from what may be assumed by a third
party. For example, one might differentiate
and identify independent study, field
experience learning, internships, and
cooperative education.[6]

6.32 Transcripts should include additional
information as may be necessary to make
clear the nature of the learning represented.
Other information that may be relevant
to particular types of learning includes:
dates when learning was assessed so that
third parties might better judge whether
learning is still current; details such as
location, supervision, or duration, which
may bear upon quality of learning; an
indication of how the learning was documented and assessed and what standards
were employed.

---

[6] When the credits that are awarded are expressed in terms of explicitly stated learning
outcomes, this procedure (6.31) should not be necessary. *Ideally* all transcripts would
describe the level and content of skills and knowledge acquired (i.e., the learning
outcomes). The sources of the learning would be irrelevant. *Realistically*, however,
many consumers of transcript information still base important decisions on their
perceptions of the *source* of learning, rather than exclusively on its level and content.
Until this practice disappears it would be unfair to learners if the source of learning
were not specified on the transcript.

Chapter Five
Administrative Measures to Safeguard Quality Assurance

"It is not enough to have quality. Quality also has to be maintained and guaranteed. In higher education, *quality assurance* is the collective term for institutional activities, policies, and procedures that provide a measure of confidence that what is done academically is consistent with the institution's goals and is likely to effect learning at levels established by the institution or by external bodies."[1]

It isn't possible to draw a sharp line between the *academic* **standards** addressed above and the *administrative* **standards** that are the subject of this chapter. Many of the administrative priniciples and procedures enumerated below appear also in the discussion of academic principles and procedures for sponsored and prior experiential learning assessment.

There are, however, additional administrative threads in the fabric of quality assurance. These relate particularly to **Standards VII, VIII, IX,** and **X** (publication of policies, cost of assessment, training of assessors, and program evaluation).

Standard VI (avoid duplication) is covered in the preceding chapters (3.5 in sponsored learning and 5.41 in prior learning). Administrative safeguards for observance of this **standard** should be included in the development of each institution's administrative policies and procedures.

The administrative principles and procedures in the following summary are not offered as sequential steps extending the 6 Steps in each of the sections on academic principles and procedures. They are,

---

[1] Jane Kendall, in *Strengthening Experiential Education Within Your Institution*, p. 74. (See Reference #10 on p. 104.)

however, numbered in sequence – 7, 8, 9, and 10 – to correspond to **Standards VII, VIII, IX,** and **X.**

Step 7: Principles and procedures related to Standard VII:

"Policies and procedures applied to assessment, including provision for appeal, should be fully disclosed and prominently available."

Programs that depart significantly from traditional educational activities bear a special responsibility to facilitate a clear understanding of the program. This applies both to philosophy and to implementation. The need is partly to justify and legitimize the program and partly to help interested parties to see how it works. The philosophy underlying experiential learning programs needs to be reflected in formal policy. (A model for a comprehensive policy is included as Appendix D.) The effective implementation of policy requires both its publication in appropriate places and the development of supporting procedures and the distribution of a statement about them. This task includes coordination among a wide range of campus documents including: the official catalog, faculty manual, instruction booklets and guidelines, program flyers and other advertising, and forms used by faculty and students.

Articulate Rationale	7.1 Institutions should articulate a clear rationale for fostering and crediting experiential learning, especially as it may bear upon the nature of the institution's degrees or its mission.
Include Faculty in the Process	7.2 The definition of institutional policies and procedures concerning assessment and crediting of experiential learning should involve faculty, students, and others as appropriate and should receive formal review and approval through the regular academic procedures of the institution.
	7.21 There should be a designated administrator with clear responsibility for seeing that all institutional policies and guidelines concerning assessment of experiential learning are properly observed.

**Clarify
Relationship of
Experiential
Programs to
Degrees**

7.3 Insofar as possible in traditional as well as nontraditional programs, requirements for postsecondary degrees should be stated as reasonably specific types of knowledge, competence, capability, disposition, or other well-defined educational outcomes rather than in general terms or in terms of some specific number of courses or units.

7.31 Faculty should examine systematically what types of experiential learning can contribute most effectively to attainment of degree requirements.

**Integrate with
Other Programs**

7.4 It is important to clarify how experiential learning programs operate in relation to other components of the institution and to ensure that policies and procedures are well-integrated with those of other departments and functions.

7.41 It is useful to develop an operational model that describes how an experiential learning program operates within the institution.

**Clarify Roles and
Responsibilities**

7.5 Roles and responsibilities of all persons connected with the assessment (including students) should be clarified, and a written description of such roles and responsibilities should be provided to all involved.

**Recognize
Diversity of
Student Body**

7.6 As necessary, assessment services and degree planning activities should be available at unconventional times and places in order to accommodate needs of students engaged in nontraditional patterns of learning. The quality of such services should be equal to that of the services provided for the student who is on the traditional daytime track.

Protect Individual Privacy

7.7 There should be established procedures regarding the handling and filing of student portfolios and other materials related to assessment in order to protect the privacy of students and others as appropriate.

Provide Written Guidelines

7.8 Even though an experiential learning program may be small and program practices may be well understood by those involved in it, conscientiously prepared written guidelines are important for several reasons. It is only through written guidelines that public scrutiny can assure proper accountability. Also, written statements provide the necessary reference to ensure that policies are interpreted and applied consistently. Written guidelines greatly facilitate the efficiency of faculty and students who are new to the program.

7.81 It is highly desirable that institutions provide a comprehensive faculty handbook describing policies and practices for all programs involving assessment and crediting of experiential learning. Desirable components of such a handbook include all documents and descriptions to which the **standards** in this book refer, but especially those on program rationale, assessment procedures, standards employed, crediting policies, and evidence of quality assurance in assessment.

7.82 There should be an appropriate descriptive brochure for students considering participation in any experiential pro-

gram or assessment of prior learning. This
descriptive material should contain sufficient information to permit students to
make an informed judgment as to whether
participation is likely to prove useful, cost-
effective, and worth the student's time.

7.83 Students participating in a sponsored
program or in a program for prior learning
assessment should be provided with an
integrated set of descriptive materials,
forms, and supporting documents that
provide complete information about
program procedures and policies.

7.84 Program administrators must make
sure that there is "truth in advertising," and
that students are not misled about costs,
about the time and effort required, or about
the amount of credit that they will earn.
Under no circumstances should there be
any implied promises that any credit will
be awarded.

Step 8: Principles and procedures related to Standard VIII:
*"Fees charged for assessment should be based on the services performed
in the process and not solely determined by the amount of credit awarded."*
Financing is a critical aspect of assessing experiential learning
with respect to both cost effectiveness and pricing. The highly individual character of experiential learning often necessitates assessment
that is tailored to an individual's specific learning. Consequently,
some forms of assessment may be technically desirable but prohibi-
tively expensive. Also, pricing assessment and accounting for its cost
raises a host of administrative questions that are vital to a program's
operation and success. Thus, choice of assessment method must take
cost into account, and vice versa.

Ensure Cost   8.1 Institutions should ensure through
Effectiveness   careful analysis of direct and indirect costs
                         that procedures for assessing experiential

learning are cost-effective with respect to the interests of students, the institution, and broader social considerations.

8.11 Care should be taken to allocate costs of assessment and its financing in ways that are equitable to students as consumers and to faculty as providers.

Recognize Assessment As Instruction

8.2 Analysis of the cost of assessment should take into proper account all instructional functions it serves; a sound assessment procedure should not be sacrificed simply because it appears superficially more expensive than traditional assessment methods. The fact that assessment of experiential learning is often closely connected with the instructional process suggests that its cost effectiveness should be evaluated on a different basis from that of most educational assessment. If assessment of experiential learning is designed to have direct educational benefit, its financing might well be considered to be partly an instructional cost. For field preparation courses, concurrent or follow-up seminars, and for prior learning assessment orientation courses, there is a direct opportunity to relate instruction and assessment.

8.21 Remuneration to assessors of prior learning should not be based upon the number of credit hours awarded.

Relate Costs Accurately to Consumer Value

8.3 Special assessment procedures should be worth what they cost the student; prices should be equitable in relation to actual cost of assessment and the real benefit of the assessment process itself. Assessment of prior learning must not be, or appear to be, a means of buying credits.

Monitor Cost Efficiency

8.4 Institutions should constantly work to improve the management and efficiency of assessment procedures so as to improve cost effectiveness without reducing the quality of assessment or its usefulness to individual students.

Step 9: Principles and procedures related to Standard IX:

"All personnel involved in the assessment of learning should receive adequate training for the functions they perform, and there should be provision for their continued professional development."

Prerequisite to providing adequate training for assessors, the institution must (1) decide who is involved in the process, and (2) define roles and specify responsibilities for all of the parties. In addition to the learner there are often several other persons involved in assessment who might rightly be termed assessors. They serve several functions which may or may not be performed by the same individual. These include: (a) mentoring or helping the student define and pursue learning and assessment objectives; (b) making judgments about the character and level of learning; and (c) determining the value of learning in credits or other academic currency. For present purposes an assessor is anyone who regularly performs either of the latter two functions on behalf of the institution.

Identify Assessors and Their Roles

9.1 Assessors who make regular evaluations of student learning are to be distinguished from other resource persons who may provide information or be consulted only occasionally regarding assessment; e.g., subject matter experts or work supervisors.

9.11 Any responsible person may possibly qualify as an expert or assessment resource person if the individual brings objectivity and appropriate special knowledge to the assessment task. There is a variety of

evidence that can qualify an individual as
an expert: publications or awards, recommendations of other experts, professional
position, etc.

9.12 It is very desirable to develop a clear
rationale as to what types of assessors are to
be used in an experiential learning program. Assessors can be subject matter
experts, assessment experts, or faculty
concerned with generic competences not
associated with a particular discipline. They
may or may not include individuals outside
the institution. The role of outside experts,
however, should be confined to judgments
concerning knowledge and competence
levels attained. The determination of credit
awards must be made by faculty members
of the institution awarding the credit.
Policies regarding choice of assessors
should reflect the nature of the program
and the types of learning involved.

9.13 Whenever necessary a team of assessors should be utilized in order to obtain
the knowledge and expertise that may be
required to assess adequately the learning
in question.

Specify
Responsibilities
of Assessors

9.2 The responsibilities of assessors, experts,
and other assessment resource persons
should be clearly specified.

9.21 It is highly desirable that appropriate
instructions and reference materials be
readily available to faculty concerning
technical procedures for any assessment
method that has significant use and is
different from routine testing and grading.

9.22 It is desirable to develop a clear sequence of steps for guiding students through the assessment process. A flow diagram showing how the student proceeds through steps and decision points may be especially helpful in describing the process.

Establish Qualifications for Assessors

9.3 Assessors should be competent not only in the subject matter of their assessment but also in the principles and limitations of the assessment technique employed.

9.31 Assessors and other resource persons should be unbiased and objective with respect to both personal knowledge of the student and the learning involved.

Provide Adequate Training for Assessors

9.4 The responsible administrator and principal assessors in the institution should make every effort to be sure that all individuals who are charged with responsibilities connected with assessment have received training appropriate to those responsibilities.

9.41 Important training objectives include understanding the effective use of experiential learning, how to select and adapt assessment methods, how better to define learning objectives and write appropriate evaluations of outcomes, how to enhance accuracy of assessment, and how to interpret standards in awarding credit.

9.42 It is very important to give new assessors supervised experience in assessing learning and awarding credit in order to ensure that they do not inadvertently set their own judgmental standards too leniently or too conservatively in relation to institutional guidelines.

9.43 All persons involved in any aspect of the assessment process should be acquainted with relevant experiential learning provisions of the regional accrediting association and of any specialized accrediting bodies that may be involved.

Step 10: Principles and procedures related to Standard X:
"Assessment programs should be regularly monitored, reviewed, evaluated, and revised as needed to reflect changes in the needs being served and in the state of the assessment arts."

To lock quality assurance into place it is essential for good assessment practice to have three characteristics: sound conception, effective execution, and systematic program evaluation. The previous nine sections have been largely concerned with the conception and execution of assessment procedures. Quality assurance relies critically on the third characteristic: systematic program evaluation. This includes monitoring adherence to good practices, improving effectiveness, and use of the best procedures for accomplishing both.

Foster Professional Standards

10.1 Standards of professional practice in assessment should be appropriate to the assessment method employed. In the assessment of experiential learning it is especially important to foster a strong sense of collegial quality control as well as routine exercise of administrative responsibility. Objective examinations and other standardized assessment instruments should be evaluated on the basis of detailed specifications and empirical evidence regarding the characteristics of the instruments, especially their reliability and validity for the purposes they are to serve. Such specifications and evidence constitute a principal safeguard for ensuring quality and minimizing abuse. The corollary safeguard in expert judgment of experiential learning lies in faculty consensus regarding policy, peer review of practices, appropriate authentication, and systematic review of day-to-day program operation.

10.11 An appropriate official at the institution should have clearly designated responsibility for monitoring the quality of assessment procedures.

10.12 A basic precept of quality assurance is that assessment practices are improved by systematic study of the results of assessment, including studies of agreement among faculty on interpretation of assessment policies and consistency in the outcomes of assessment.

10.13 There should be periodic review of assessment procedures and of information pertaining thereto, preferably involving an objective and informed outsider plus representatives of those who routinely participate in assessment. One purpose of such review should be to note any marked discrepancy between the assessment policy or results of assessment and those of other institutions. The occurence of such discrepancies should be an occasion for examining the rationale of institutional policy and practice.

Seek Agreement on Practices

10.2 It is desirable to determine periodically whether there is reasonable faculty agreement regarding institutional policy as to what learning is college level and what learning is creditable against particular degree objectives. Available evidence indicates that substantial faculty disagree-

ment is common and that institutional
standards may fluctuate. Written guidelines, faculty development activities, and
routine checks on agreement are normally
necessary in order to achieve and maintain
satisfactory consensus on such issues.

10.21 Periodic checks should be made to
ensure that assessors are adhering to
institutional assessment guidelines and
procedures.

Monitor Authenticity

10.3 The authenticity of different types of
documentation should be checked on a
periodic basis.

10.31 Students should be apprised of
authentication procedures.

10.32 If self-reports of learning are involved
as a part of the process, periodic checks
should be made to ensure that there is
adequate faculty verification before credit is
awarded.

Monitor Consistency in Assessment

10.4 Institutions should establish routine
procedures for periodically examining the
consistency of assessment judgments and
credit awards. When judges subscribe to
common principles and guidelines, there is
a strong tendency to assume reasonable
consistency in judgments from judge to
judge and from time to time. Ample
evidence indicates, however, that such
consistency is often not found. It is essential
to verify adequate consistency in order to
ensure that assessments are fair. The most
dependable way to make such a verification
is to undertake a special study in which the
same assessments are carried out twice

through usual procedures (but quite independently) and then compared for consistency.

10.41 Examination of the consistency of assessment results should contribute to judgments as to the adequacy of assessment procedures and the competence of assessors. For example, analyses of assessment results should provide answers to such questions as the following: (a) Are any assessors consistently unable to agree reasonably well with other assessors? (b) Do assessment outcomes indicate that reasonably consistent agreement is seldom possible with respect to particular assessment methods or types of learning? (c) Is there any indication that particular assessors or classes of assessors are consistently more or less lenient in applying standards and principles?

10.42 Particular assessors or methods of assessment should not be used if evidence indicates that assessment is not measuring what is intended or if assessments are frequently unreliable or if some students do not appear to be fairly assessed.

10.43 Analyses of the degree of consistency between two independent sets of assessments should take proper account of the fact that a high percentage agreement between judges can occur merely because both pass a similar percentage of students. Two types of disagreement between assessors must be distinguished. Assessors can disagree on the standard they impose (i.e., what percent pass) or in the choice of which individual they judge to meet the standard. The latter is normally considered a much more dependable basis for deciding whether assessments are reasonably consistent.

Employ Appropriate Technical Procedures

10.5 Standard methods of educational measurement and correlational statistics should be employed in evaluating validity and reliability of procedures for assessing experiential learning.

10.51 Technical procedures employed and samples of faculty and students used to determine validity and reliability of assessment should be described sufficiently to permit judgment as to the representativeness and the stability of the results. Any decisions regarding assessment procedures that are based on such data should be reached in consultation with faculty who have appropriate training in the technical aspects of educational measurement.

Monitor Value to Students

10.6 Periodic checks should be made to determine whether students feel that assessment procedures are sound and equitable and whether the institution is fulfilling satisfactorily commitments made concerning experiential learning programs.

10.61 Special effort should be exerted to determine in what ways the assessment process can be made more beneficial to the student's self-development and self-awareness of personal competence. Whenever possible, it is desirable to evaluate alternate methods of assessment with these objectives in mind.

Schedule Periodic Program Evaluations

10.7 In addition to formative evaluation and improvement, experiential learning programs and related assessment procedures should undergo periodic summative evaluation of overall effectiveness, efficiency, and continuing usefulness in their current form. Judgments concerning the quality and effectiveness of nontraditional educational programs and assessment procedures should be made in the context of comparable information concerning traditional programs.

Chapter Six
Misconceptions and Malpractice

Malpractice is sometimes the direct result of misconceptions. For example, there is a common misconception that confuses inputs with outcomes and equates experience with learning. Not surprisingly, there is a common malpractice of awarding credit in internships and other work study programs primarily (or even exclusively) on the basis of number of hours per week spent on the job. Such credit awards are based more on the amount of learning *activity* (input) than on the level or quality of learning *results* (outcomes).

For the most part, however, the negative results of misconceptions and malpractices are independent of each other. The worst problem with *misconceptions* (such as the nine described below) is that they inhibit the development of effective experiential learning programs. In the worst case they actually lead to termination of existing programs or the disapproval of new proposals.

The problem with different kinds of *malpractice* (such as the eight described below) is that they endanger the quality of experiential learning programs. In the worst cases, they are thoroughly unprofessional and unethical; e.g., as with the exchange of profits for credits or the selling of degrees.

A successful program requires formal periodic review of both concept and practice. The nine misconceptions and the eight kinds of malpractice described here are samples of the worst in each category. To establish a sound basis for quality control it is appropriate to amend this list to reflect locally-relevant impediments to effective recognition of experiential learning.

A. Nine Misconceptions

#1. "Credit for prior learning depresses enrollments."

This is a particularly unfortunate misconception because the truth is exactly the opposite: professionally responsible assessment of prior learning facilitates access and encourages enrollment. Older potential students (and it is the older student, more often than the younger and less experienced traditional student, who is most likely to have creditable experiential learning) are much more likely to enroll if they can get appropriate recognition for their experiential learning and thus avoid repetitive learning.

An excellent cure for this misconception is communication with adult learners—potential, current, and already graduated. Often they are, or are willing to be, enrolled as students precisely because of prior learning assessment opportunities.

#2. "Challenge exams (credit by examination) are acceptable; portfolio-assisted assessments are not."

This misconception is no doubt fueled by the prevalence of various forms of malpractice—e.g.; improper uses of portfolios. The misconception is also related to misunderstanding of what portfolios really are. The truth is that a properly administered portfolio-assisted assessment is more rigorous than a challenge exam and may even include one or more traditional written and/or oral examinations. Portfolios can, in fact, quite appropriately be described as "examinations of last resort." The portfolio process was created to cover those instances (understandably very common in experiential learning) where the boundaries of the learning do not correspond with the boundaries that define catalog courses or generally available standardized examinations.

Patterns of experiential learning are unique to the individual learner. Portfolio processes represent uniquely individualized assessments. We cannot afford, across-the-board, the luxury of such individualized, in-depth assessment for every student in every classroom. If we could, it would be fair to conclude that portfolio-assisted assessment might well be the preferred "examination" for all learning.

Before the misconception about portfolios can be laid to rest, however, it must be conceded that there are both acceptable and quite unacceptable approaches to portfolio assessment. Responsible portfolio programs are as good as, or better than, most challenge examinations. They may (in fact, ought to) even include challenge exams as part of the process whenever they fit the circumstances. The possibility of malpractice in the use of portfolios should not be permitted to diminish the perceived validity of a form of examination that is uniquely fitted to, and essential for, the assessment of experiential learning.

#3. "It is improper to offer both credit and pay for experiential learning that takes place on-the-job."

This misconception is often heard in the discussion of internships, cooperative education assignments, and other work-and-learn programs. Unfortunately it is almost as persistent as it is illogical. The roots of the misconception are found in the common confusion of experiential activities and learning outcomes. In fact, the pay is primarily for one, while the credit is for the other. Paid internships are not only legitimate but are a particularly excellent way to combine the acquisition of learning with its financing. The experiential activity for which pay may be offered by the employer is an input; the experiential learning for which credit may be awarded by the campus is an outcome.

The evaluation of learning and the award of credit for it ought to be a separate process from the acquisition of learning. Even in so-called traditional classrooms different students learn in different ways—some more from reading, some more from listening, some more from experimenting, some more from writing, and some more from discussion. In experiential learning it does not make any sense to differentiate between the learning of volunteers and the learning of paid workers if a valid assessment indicates that they have learned the same thing.

#4. "Only full-time faculty on regular appointments are qualified to determine credit awards for experiential learning."

Whether this, in fact, is a misconception or a questionable practice is not entirely clear. It is sometimes adopted as a practice in reaction to malpractice. (See, for example, #4 in the list of types of malpractice which follows.) What needs to be kept in mind is that two types of expertise are required for determining levels of competence and awarding credit. Competent assessment requires expertise both in the subject matter *content* and in the assessment *process*. (**Standard IV.**)

The misconception that only full-time faculty members possess both of these qualities is a classic case of confusing the "necessary" with the "sufficient." Full-time, regularly appointed faculty status certainly ought to be *sufficient* to guarantee both content and process expertise in the faculty member's area of specialization. And it should be all that is *necessary* in traditional programs dealing with classroom learning and conventional examination processes. Experiential learning, however, characteristically crosses disciplinary boundaries and requires individualized assessment. A single faculty member may be qualified in part of the content and in part of the appropriate assessment procedure but not necessarily in all of either.

The required expertise, either for content or for process, may very likely be found in persons who are neither full-time nor regularly appointed.

What is important to remember as a safeguard for quality assurance is that both kinds of expertise must be applied. Either, or both, may exist without regard to the faculty appointment status of the experts.

#5. "Credit for prior experiential learning should not be recorded on the transcript until after the student has demonstrated proof of ability to succeed by passing thirty units of traditional coursework."

Whether this is really a misconception is debatable. It appears to have two roots. First, it reflects lack of confidence in the portfolio process and superimposes on it a sort of "doublecheck." It is not a complete verification process because it only works when it gets negative results. If it is proven that the student isn't capable of college-level learning, then the portfolio process must have been flawed. But if it is demonstrated, by success in the traditional classroom, that the student can do college work, it doesn't necessarily validate the portfolio assessment but merely indicates that it *could* have been valid.

The second source of this verification practice is more logical. It is the feeling that the primary mission of the postsecondary institution is to teach, not to assess what may have been learned elsewhere. By establishing a waiting period for recording the results of prior learning assessment, the learner is denied the possibility of "using" the institution as a convenient assessor. The institution's desire to avoid the "pure assessor" role is met, at least partially, by another rule: making prior learning assessment available only to enrolled students. That rule is, in fact, almost universal. However, it doesn't prevent students from enrolling temporarily, and with the primary purpose of prior learning assessment. A deterrent to this bypass is the reluctance (often outright refusal) of institutions to accept prior learning credits for transfer.

Postsecondary institutions do, of course, have the right to determine their own missions. If they want to be exclusively teaching institutions that is their prerogative. It is a quite reasonable position to take with respect to students who are seeking their degrees elsewhere but simply want to use one institution as an assessor of credits to transfer to another. For their own degree-seeking students, however, colleges and universities should (and most do) recognize that some college-level learning may take place outside the academy prior to enrollment. To delay the recording of that learning serves no purpose except verification, and that—as noted above—is only partially effective at best.

In defense of delayed transcribing, it has to be noted that for continuing students who are going to complete at least 30 units anyway it isn't really any hardship to have the recording delayed. Nevertheless the existence of such a rule probably does more harm than good. It stands primarily as a statement of doubt about an assessment process that ought to be given full recognition if it is professionally administered and simply disallowed if it is not.

#6. "Only courses taken on campus should be accepted for residence credit."

This statement is burdened by two questionable assumptions: *first*, that campus courses **always** achieve some essential added value from being taken within a community of scholars; and *second*, that learning acquired elsewhere **never** provides this advantage.

The ultimate failure of these conclusions is perhaps best illustrated by the phenomenon of "concurrent enrollment" which permits matriculated and non-matriculated students to enroll in the same class, on the campus, but grants residence credit to one and denies it to the other.

Both sides of this residency argument are weak. The argument that there is something special and essential to be gained from immersion in a community of scholars is difficult to defend on commuter campuses. Many working students rush onto campus just before class and depart immediately afterwards. It might as well have happened a hundred miles away. There is no leisurely discussion over a cup of coffee, no sitting on a bench in the quad chatting with an instructor (or even a fellow student), not even an opportunity to drop in at "office hours" to ask a question, and no time to take advantage of a "brown bag" appearance by a visiting scholar.

On the other side of the question it isn't necessarily accurate to conclude that the prior learner was totally denied the advantages of a community of scholars. Ours is a mobile community. Scholars are found in the workplace, at off-campus dinner parties, in the family, and regularly in the media (sometimes even with interactive capability).[1]

It can't be denied that "real" residency (i.e., living on campus) offers more opportunity for informal participation in a community of scholars than is enjoyed by commuting students and by most off-campus experiential learners. But the rules for computing the residency advantage are faulty. A redefinition is long overdue. The presumed advantage of immersion in the community of scholars should be described in terms that permit its measurement. *Where* learning takes place and *how* it takes place are not adequate yardsticks. If "x" amount of residency is to be a basic degree requirement (and it does seem to be a potentially defensible idea), then its advantages and the conditions for realizing them should be specified and enforced. Only then will it be possible to determine how much the circumstances of prior experiential learning may have contributed toward the realization of the residency goals.

#7. "Prior learning credit should be granted only when its content corresponds to that of courses listed in the catalog."

Whether this is misconception or borderline malpractice is not clear. What is clear, however, is that the idea is imposed as a barrier to the award of credit for prior learning, and that it is a very weak rule. Essentially it is an attempt to impose a double standard, denying credit for prior learning in subjects for which credit is regularly granted for campus-sponsored learning. There are three common ways in which credit is granted for learning not described in a catalog

---

[1] Many "external" degree programs have been fully accredited by the regional associations. A national organization, The ALLIANCE, has been created to serve the needs of alternative degree programs for adults. A set of "principles of good practice" for external degree programs has been developed. Information about The ALLIANCE is available from: Director of Adult Degree Program, Mary Baldwin College, Stanton, VA 24401.

course: transfer credit from other institutions; credit for independent study; and credit in "variable topic" courses. The same rules that permit credit for these three sources of learning should be applicable for prior experiential learning. The important rules for quality assurance purposes are described above in **Academic Standards I** through **V**: credit should be granted for college-level learning with an appropriate balance of theory and application, as determined by qualified experts.

#8. "Credit for experiential learning should not be granted at the graduate level."

Again it is difficult to draw a sharp line between misconception and questionable practice. The vigorous opposition that exists toward experiential learning at the graduate level appears to be primarily protectionist, based on the fear that credit for prior learning will depress enrollments, endanger quality assurance, or do both. The opposition also reflects the conviction that graduate learning is somehow so different that it cannot be found anywhere except in the graduate school. Finally, it appears to reflect the same lack of confidence in external sources of learning that is characteristic in some graduate schools' reluctance to grant transfer credit even to traditional learning from accredited graduate schools.

All of these strands of resistance to experiential learning credit are belied by the actual practices of most graduate schools. While they are belligerently opposed to the idea of granting credit for external learning they actually do a lot of it, but under another name. Waivers are granted for specific subjects, substitutions are permitted, and alternate methods of satisfying requirements are accepted. Behind the rigid rule there is a pattern of flexible process that often does, in fact, take accurate account of prior learning. Repetitive learning is not usually required. But what results is a *change* in the requirements rather than a *reduction*. The graduate degree becomes a "value added" degree rather than a chronicle of competence. Award of a graduate degree thus tends to be distorted, accurately reflecting the achievement of at least *enough* competence, but failing to record the *overfulfillment* that results for those who enter the program with graduate level prior learning that is not allowed to satisfy local requirements.

What is needed at both the graduate and undergraduate levels is for degrees to be defined in terms of learning outputs, i.e., competence in specified knowledge and skills. Otherwise the academic degrees are inflated currency, distorted by misconceived overemphasis on inputs and failing to reflect what they are supposed to be all about: generally acceptable evidence of specified levels and amounts of learning.

#9. "Advanced placement, without credit, and waivers of requirement are reasonable alternatives to credit for prior experiential learning."

Like the graduate school practice this one at the undergraduate level has unfair results that skew the meaning of the baccalaureate degree. Unlike the graduate version of the "value added" approach, however, the waiver and advanced placement (without credit) options at the undergraduate level have been formalized and made temptingly easy for faculty and administrators to apply. Probably the worst violation of fairness and logic occurs with respect to foreign language credit. Those with significant competence in a second language are routinely placed in appropriate advanced classes, but also routinely denied credit for their recognized competence. It is a pure case of the "value added" distortion of the meaning of the baccalaureate degree. A degree requirement expressed as "fluency in a second language" is reasonable and fairly common. It is hard to deny its contemporary utility. But if the student with a language headstart of 6 or more units is required to "make up" those six units by taking additional electives the meaning of the degree is distorted. That student has *overfulfilled* the requirements, reaching the same level as is required of all students in the foreign language area and completing six units more than other students in the elective category. It is one more piece of evidence that degrees ought to be defined in terms of competency rather than of "time served."

B. Eight Kinds of Malpractice

#1. Basing assessment fees on the number of credits awarded.

In its worst form this practice is accurately described as the selling of degrees. The widely publicized "diploma mills" often combine this error with the violation of other standards—particularly the granting of credit for experience, rather than learning. (See Malpractice #2, below.) Neither problem, however, is confined to the non-accredited malpractice community.

The "fees per credit awarded" procedure has two serious negative results: it inaccurately reflects the true costs of assessment; and it injects profit motive into a decision that should be made on purely academic grounds. The real cost of assessment may be as great for a *no credit* decision as for a more positive finding. It may make sense to set fees in terms of units *assessed*, but not in terms of units *awarded*. It is virtually the same as the cost relationship between "pass" and "fail" in traditional classroom settings. Tuition pays for units attempted, not units completed.

The negative influence of profit motivation can be either personal or institutional. It is most serious in the case of the "for profit" institutions. It can be a serious problem in any situation where the assessor's reward is dependent on the number of units granted. The only way to guarantee quality in the award of academic credit is to ensure that the charges for assessment are, in fact, charges for the cost of assessment and not for the award of credit.

#2. Credit is granted for "time served."
Probably the most widespread violation of **Standard I** (credit should be granted only for learning, not experience) is automatic credit for military service. The award level was commonly set at 9 semester units for a year and a day of enlisted service, and 15 units for a year and a day of commissioned service. The practice was almost universal in the years immediately following World War I and was continued by many after World War II. Fortunately it is being replaced in most institutions with a more appropriate provision that grants credit for *learning* as recommended by the *Guide to the Evaluation of Educational Experience in the Armed Services* (American Council on Education).

As noted in the preceding section the worst continuing form of malpractice associated with credit for experience is in institutions that are not accredited by an agency recognized by either the U.S. Department of Education or the Council on Postsecondary Accreditation (COPA). Some actually advertise the awarding of "credit for life experiences" and grant it, for a price, without ascertaining that learning resulted from the experience.

There are some violations of **Standard I** in accredited institutions—particularly in field work assignments where direct relationships are established between "hours of work per week" and "credits granted for the field experience." A similar violation, credit for "seat time," sometimes occurs in traditional classroom courses where a percentage of the final grade is based on attendance.

#3. Promises of credit that is "likely" to be awarded.

Even in institutions where substantial care is taken to grant credit for learning, not experience, a careless approach to advertising often *implies* that a credit award is likely. Once the applicant's expectations have been raised by catchy brochure phrases (e.g., "your life experience can earn college credit"), assessors may be put on the defensive and have a difficult time enforcing the **standards**. Care should be taken to avoid publicizing such encouraging observations as "you can earn as much as thirty units for your life experience learning", or "portfolio students average fourteen units of credit", etc.

It is not easy to prepare a portfolio. Good institutional practice requires that information materials reflect, up front, the facts that: credit is only granted for learning; the student is required to invest significant time and effort in making the case that experience has, in fact, resulted in college-creditable learning; it is not possible to know in advance whether (or, if so, how much) credit may be awarded; and the final determination of credit awards will be based on expert measurement and evaluation of that learning.

#4. Incompetent assessment and evaluation.

When institutions yield to the temptation to save money, time, or effort by relying on insufficiently prepared assessors, they violate **Standard IV**. This **standard** requires that both the assessment and the evaluation of learning must be accomplished by persons with relevant expertise in the subject matter *content* and in the assessment *process*. It is possible to find a single person, usually a faculty member, who embodies both kinds of expertise. The temptation to cut corners (and thus to save money) is common in assessing and evaluating experiential learning because the subject matter often cuts across disciplinary boundaries thus requiring the services of more than one subject matter expert. Another common temptation is to accept the credit recommendation of non-faculty experts whose expertise is limited to the subject matter and is insufficient on assessment techniques or in determination of the academic meaning and value of a particular competence.

Incompetent assessment is sometimes actually the result of misguided, though sincere, attempts to be objective. "Objectivity" is sought by avoiding contact between assessor and learner. The entire process may be completed by mail. The virtues of anonymity are realized, but the probing advantages of personal contact are lost. The assessment deficiency that results may be in either direction: the award of credit that is not deserved; or the failure to uncover, and give appropriate credit for, learning that the isolated petitioner didn't recognize or report.

Another source of assessment error may be the triple-headed pitfall of "atomization, mechanization, and bureaucratization." With "atomization"—breaking the portfolio into measurable parts—there is the danger of losing some of the essential connective tissue. The measuring, however accurate, of small details may overshadow the assessment of more important generic capabilities. This negative phenomenon may be extended by an attempt to ensure efficiency by "mechanizing"—breaking the process into parts before identifying the "syndrome" that is needed to hold them together in a meaningful whole. Both atomization and mechanization result from a "bureaucratization" of the process that seems efficient and useful in dealing with regulatory authority.

The worst violations probably occur when outside entrepreneurs are involved in assisting with the development of the portfolio, including recommendations for credit. Institutions that accept recommendations from this source run heavy risk of double malpractice: insufficient expertise exacerbated by credit-inflating profit motives.

#5. Credit is granted for incomplete learning; necessary theoretical or practical components are missing.

The proper balance between theory and applied learning varies with the subject matter. Malpractice in this area can involve the absence of either essential balancing component. The theory expert who has no practical learning is the classic failure of much traditional education. On the other hand, the practical expert with insufficient theoretical understanding is often a handicapped learner when it comes to applying the experiential learning in new settings or to explaining to somebody else how something works. It is appropriate to grant credit for either component if the other has been, or will be, completed as an integral part of the learning plan. The most common violation in the assessment of experiential learning is to grant credit for practical competence disregarding theoretical knowledge that may be essential to properly balanced learning.

#6. Credit is granted for competences that have already been appropriately recognized—or will be in completing other requirements of the learning plan.

Adequate safeguards against duplication of credit are often lacking. It is sometimes difficult, particularly when dealing with interdisciplinary learning, to detect double crediting. It is not possible, even in a traditional environment, to eliminate all of the overlap that occurs between courses. It is essential, however, to establish duplication checkpoints at a sufficiently administrative level to assure effective monitoring. Otherwise an assessment that follows all other **standards** for quality assurance may violate **Standard VI**: credit awards should be monitored to avoid duplication.

#7. Credit is granted for progress, rather than for attaining college-level learning.

This is a common malpractice in assessing learning, both in the traditional classroom and in experiential learning programs. It is possible to make a great deal of progress, but still not achieve a level of competence that is appropriate for college credit. What makes it difficult to eliminate this malpractice is that *progress* is a thoroughly commendable learning objective. In fact the best of all possible educational worlds would be the one in which all individuals are helped to learn all that it is possible and appropriate for them to learn—taking accurate account of where they start and how far they are capable of going. What amounts to malpractice is to confuse progress, however commendable, with achievement of certified levels of competence. The "D" student may have made more progress during the class than the "A" student—having started at a much lower point. However, to base the grade on the amount of progress destroys its meaning. The idea of *"A" for effort* should not be applied to transcripts and diplomas that are alleged to carry a different message reflecting *levels* of learning rather than *new amounts* of learning.

#8. Credit for experiential learning is granted only in the major and not in general education (or, only in general education and not in the major).

Improper rules that restrict credit for experiential learning to certain categories of degree requirements are common. They violate good practice because they constitute a double standard—crediting traditional learning but denying credit to identical learning from experiential sources. There is no way to view rules like this except as indirect attempts to deny credit for extracollegiate experiential learning. For example, if experiential learning credit is acceptable only for required courses, or only for the major, or only for general education, it is denied for free electives. Yet virtually all baccalaureate degrees include free electives. There are favorite whipping horses like basketweaving and recreational sports. It is easy enough to whip up a strong tide of disapproval for granting college credit to students because they are good swimmers or handy at crafts. But if these same competences are, in fact, credited when acquired on the campus it is improper to exclude them from extra-campus experiential learning.

A Concluding Note

Misconceptions sometimes impede the development of the experiential learning programs that are needed for effective services in postsecondary institutions. Various kinds of malpractice endanger the quality of assessment and evaluation—both in traditional and experiential programs.

The misconceptions and malpractices described above, and others that may be found in local circumstances, can be countered effectively by careful adherence to the **Ten Standards** that are listed in the frontispiece of this book. By following the principles and procedures listed in Chapters Three, Four and Five, with appropriate adaptations to serve local program requirements, colleges and universities can make certain that their learning programs meet acceptable standards of quality.

References

#1. American Council on Education, Office on Educational Credit and Credentials, *Model Policy on Awarding Credit for Extrainstitutional Learning.* American Council on Education, One Dupont Circle, Washington, D.C. 20036, 1985.

#2. Educational Testing Service (ETS), *ETS Standards for Quality and Fairness*, Educational Testing Service, Princeton, New Jersey 08541, 1987.

#3. Duley, John S., *Learning Outcomes: The Measurement and Evaluation of Experiential Learning*, PANEL Resource Paper #6, National Society for Internships and Experiential Education (NSIEE), 3509 Haworth #207, Ralcigh, North Carolina 27609, 1982.

#4. Kolb, David A., *The Learning Style Inventory,* McBer and Company, Boston, 1976.

#5. Keeton, Morris T., ed., *Defining and Assuring Quality in Experiential Learning,* New Directions Series #9, Jossey-Bass, San Francisco, 1980.

#6. Keeton, Morris T., and Tate, Pamela J., *learning by experience – what, why, how,* Jossey-Bass, San Francisco, 1981.

#7. Keeton, Morris T., et al., *Experiential Learning: Rationale, Characteristics and Assessment,* Jossey-Bass, San Francisco, 1976.

#8. Knapp, Joan E., and Jacobs, Paul I., *Setting Standards for Assessing Experiential Learning,* Council for Adult and Experiential Learning (CAEL), Columbia, MD, 1981.

#9. Knapp, Joan, and Sharon, Amiel, *A Compendium of Assessment Techniques,* Council for Adult and Experiential Learning (CAEL), Columbia, MD, 1975.

#10. National Society for Internships and Experiential Education (NSIEE), *Strengthening Experiential Education within Your Institution*, An NSIEE Sourcebook, NSIEE, 1983.

#11. Simosko, Susan, *Earn College Credit for What You Know*, Acropolis Books, Ltd., Washington, D.C., 1985.

#12. Simosko, Susan, et al., *Assessing Learning: A CAEL Handbook for Faculty*, Council for Adult and Experiential Learning (CAEL), Columbia, MD, 1988.

#13. Yelon, Stephen, and Duley, John S., *Efficient Evaluation of Individual Performance in Field Placement*, Michigan State University, East Lansing, Michigan 48824, 1979.

Appendix A
Checklist of Principles and Procedures for Assessing *Sponsored* Experiential Learning

Step 1. ARTICULATION: Relate learning goals to academic, personal, and professional goals.

    1.1 Determine what is creditable.
    1.2 Seek an appropriate mix of theory and applied learning.
    1.3 Define the student's learning objectives.
          1.31 Include self-awareness and personal development.
          1.32 Encourage self-directed learning.
          1.33 Use formative evaluation to revise goals as needed.
    1.4 Select learning sites compatible with learning plans.

Step 2. PLANNING: Select appropriate learning objectives and activities.

    2.1 Determine the college level of learning.
    2.2 Develop a learning plan.
          2.21 Express outcomes in terms of competences.
          2.22 Plan learning activities in anticipation of evaluation.
          2.23 Make learning objectives and activities compatible with learning style.
    2.3 Emphasize the learner's role.
    2.4 Prepare for the field experience.

Step 3. EVALUATION: Determine the credit equivalency.

    3.1 Decide who defines acceptable competences.
    3.2 Decide whether evaluation is criterion-referenced or norm-referenced.

3.21 Describe what the learner can do.

3.22 Describe the level of the learner's proficiency.

3.3 Measure outcomes, not inputs.

3.4 Apply the same standards for traditional and experiential learning.

3.5 Avoid duplication.

3.6 Credit learning, not experience.

3.7 Use learning contracts.

3.8 Integrate evaluation with current program and future plans.

3.81 Build on a foundation of prior learning assessment.

3.82 Use formative feedback.

3.83 Relate summative feedback to degree requirements and future learning.

Step 4. DOCUMENTATION: Collect evidence of learning.

4.1 Develop an institutional policy.

4.11 Include self-assessment and formative evaluation.

4.2 Specify appropriate types of documentation.

4.21 Provide students with examples.

4.22 Specify assessment purpose of each type of document.

4.3 Distinguish types of evidence.

4.31 Describe learning outcomes, not just learning activities.

4.32 Periodically review the meaning of certificates accepted as evidence of learning.

4.4 Authenticate the evidence.

4.41 Use documentation that describes the nature of the learning.

4.42 Check credibility of document authorship.

4.43 Distinguish documentation from credit recommendation.

4.5 Emphasize quality, not quantity.

Step 5. MEASUREMENT: Determine the degree and level of competence achieved.

    5.1 Fit assessment method to learning activity.
    5.2 Fit assessment method to learner.
    5.3 Utilize assessment as a learning activity.
    5.4 Ensure reliability.
        5.41 Use multiple types of assessments.
        5.42 Avoid bias and discrimination.
    5.5 Ensure validity.
        5.51 Relate outcome measurement to learning objectives.
        5.52 Use more than one type of assessment.
        5.53 Relate learning to curriculum.
    5.6 Train the assessors.
        5.61 Use detailed written procedures.
        5.62 Match assessment training to assessment method.
        5.63 Maintain consistent conditions.
    5.7 State results objectively.
    5.8 Encourage supervised self-assessment as part of the process.
        5.81 Provide for learner participation in evaluation planning.

Step 6. TRANSCRIPTION: Prepare a useful record of results.

    6.1 Communicate with third parties.
        6.11 Establish panels for review of narrative transcripts.
        6.12 Describe outcomes clearly.
    6.2 Record learning appropriately.
        6.21 Find alternatives to misleading course labels.
        6.22 Include information needed for interpretation.
        6.23 Describe outcomes.
    6.3 Describe content and level of learning.
        6.31 Identify the learning environment.
        6.32 Include dates and other significant details.

Appendix B
Checklist of Principles and Procedures for Assessing *Prior* Experiential Learning

Step 1. IDENTIFICATION: Review experience to identify potentially creditable learning.

    1.1 Determine the college level of learning.
          1.11 Specify acceptable criteria.
    1.2 Describe the learning experiences.
    1.3 Differentiate between learning and experience.
    1.4 Be specific about learning outcomes.
          1.41 Avoid credit for trivial learning outcomes.
    1.5 Consider the recency of the learning.
    1.6 Use assessment to reinforce learning.
    1.7 Use assessment to facilitate reentry and future learning.
          1.71 Provide examples of successful portfolios or other petitions for credit.
          1.72 Offer a portfolio course, or other appropriate orientation to facilitate assessment.

Step 2. ARTICULATION: Relate proposed credit to academic, personal, and professional goals.

    2.1 Determine what learning is creditable for what purposes.
    2.2 Ensure appropriate balance between theory and applied learning.
    2.3 Relate learning to student objectives.
          2.31 Integrate past learning with future learning plans.

Step 3. DOCUMENTATION: Prepare evidence to support claim for credit.

    3.1 Develop an institutional policy.
          3.11 Use documentation for a variety of purposes.
    3.2 Specify acceptable types of documentation.

       3.21 Provide students with examples.
       3.22 Specify assessment purposes of each type of document.
  3.3 Distinguish types of evidence.
       3.31 Describe learning outcomes, not just learning activities.
       3.32 Periodically review the meaning of certificates accepted as evidence of learning.
  3.4 Authenticate the evidence.
       3.41 Use documentation that describes the nature of the learning.
       3.42 Check credibility of document authorship.
       3.43 Distinguish between documentation of learning and recommendations for credit.
  3.5 Emphasize quality, not quantity.

Step 4. MEASUREMENT: Determine the degree and level of competence achieved.

  4.1 Fit the assessment method to the learning activity.
  4.2 Fit the assessment method to the learner.
  4.3 Utilize assessment as a learning activity.
  4.4 Ensure reliability.
       4.41 Use multiple types of assessment.
       4.42 Avoid bias and discrimination.
  4.5 Ensure validity.
       4.51 Relate outcome measurement to established competency descriptions if possible.
       4.52 Use a variety of assessment methods.
       4.53 Relate learning to the curriculum.
  4.6 Plan the process and train the assessors.
       4.61 Develop written procedures.
       4.62 Develop effective interview techniques.
       4.63 Be cautious in use of role-playing and simulation.
       4.64 Maintain consistent conditions for assessment.
  4.7 State the results objectively.
  4.8 Encourage supervised self-assessment as part of the process.
       4.81 Supervise self-assessment and provide adequate faculty verification.

Step 5. EVALUATION: Determine the credit equivalency.

  5.1 Determine the criteria for evaluation.
    5.11 Decide what subject matter content is creditable.
    5.12 Decide what levels of competence are required for credit.
  5.2 Decide who interprets and applies the criteria.
  5.3 Ensure equity in credit awards.
    5.31 Apply same standards for prior learning as for traditional learning.
    5.32 Measure outcomes, not inputs.
  5.4 Consider alternative types of recognition for prior learning.
    5.41 Avoid duplication of credit.
  5.5 Develop and publish credit policies.
    5.51 Credit learning, not experience.
  5.6 Provide procedures for review and appeal.
    5.61 Incorporate individual review procedures into program review plans.
  5.7 Provide timely and useful feedback.
    5.71 Explain in writing any departure from policy or procedure.
    5.72 Explain relation of awards to degree requirements.
    5.73 Use prior learning assessment as foundation for future learning plans.

Step 6. TRANSCRIPTION: Prepare a useful record of results.

  6.1 Communicate with third parties.
    6.11 Establish panels for review of narrative transcripts.
    6.12 Describe outcomes clearly.
  6.2 Record the learning appropriately.
    6.21 Find alternatives to misleading course labels.
    6.22 Include information needed for interpretation.
    6.23 Describe outcomes, not just inputs. (See 6.31 below.)
  6.3 Describe the content and level of learning.
    6.31 Describe the learning environment.
    6.32 Include dates and other significant details.

Appendix C
Checklist of Administrative Principles and Procedures for Good Practice in Assessing Experiential Learning

7. **PUBLISH POLICIES AND PRINCIPLES:**
   Make full and accurate disclosure of all rules and practices related to assessment. (See Standard VII.)

   7.1 Articulate the rationale.
   7.2 Include faculty in the process.
       7.21 Designate the responsible administrator in charge.
   7.3 Clarify relationship of experiential programs to degrees.
       7.31 Determine what learning is effective in completing requirements.
   7.4 Integrate experiential learning with other programs.
       7.41 Develop an operational model.
   7.5 Clarify roles and responsibilities.
   7.6 Respect the diversity of the student body.
   7.7 Protect individual privacy.
   7.8 Provide written guidelines.
       7.81 Develop a faculty handbook.
       7.82 Publish descriptive brochure for students.
       7.83 Develop integrated instructional and administrative materials for students.
       7.84 Ensure "truth in advertising".

8. **DEVELOP APPROPRIATE FEE SCHEDULES:**
   Fees should be based on services performed, not on credits awarded. (See Standard VIII.)

   8.1 Ensure cost effectiveness.
       8.11 Ensure equitable fees for students and pay for faculty.
   8.2 Recognize assessment as instruction.

8.21 Pay assessors for services, not for credits
awarded.

8.3 Relate cost to consumer value.

8.4 Maintain cost efficiency.

9. **PROVIDE FOR PROFESSIONAL DEVELOPMENT:
All personnel should have adequate training and
continuous opportunity for professional development.
(See Standard IX.)**

9.1 Identify assessor roles.

    9.11 Relate qualifications to responsibility.

    9.12 Recognize needs for different kinds of expertise.

    9.13 Use teams of assessors when necessary.

9.2 Specify responsibilities of assessors.

    9.21 Provide technical instruction and reference
materials.

    9.22 Develop flow diagram showing sequences of
steps in assessment process.

9.3 Establish qualifications for assessors.

    9.31 Avoid discrimination.

9.4 Provide adequate training for each type of assessment
activity.

    9.41 Define types of training needed.

    9.42 Schedule supervised experience for new
assessors.

    9.43 Inform assessors about accreditation rules.

10. **EVALUATE EXPERIENTIAL LEARNING PROGRAMS:
Programs should be regularly reviewed and revised to
maintain the state of the assessment arts. (See Standard X.)**

10.1 Foster professional standards.

    10.11 Designate review personnel.

    10.12 Study the results of assessments.

    10.13 Periodically review procedures.

10.2 Seek agreement on practices.

    10.21 Check assessors' adherence to guidelines.

10.3 Monitor authenticity.

    10.31 Inform students of procedures.

        10.32 Verify self-reports of learning.

10.4 Monitor consistency in assessment.

        10.41 Use periodic review to evaluate assessor performance.

        10.42 Discontinue use of assessors found to be unreliable.

        10.43 Distinguish between differences in agreement on standards and disagreement on their application.

10.5 Employ appropriate technical procedures.

        10.51 Make detailed analyses of results.

10.6 Monitor value to student.

        10.61 Select assessment methods that maximize self-development.

10.7 Schedule periodic program evaluations.

Appendix D
Elements of a Comprehensive Institutional Policy on Experiential Learning

This is a list of questions, rather than of answers. It is a model for a policy, rather than a sample. All of the items included are taken from the actual institutional policies of a group of accredited institutions surveyed nationwide.

In developing or revising your own institutional policy it is recommended that this list be supplemented with sample policies for other institutional environments similar to your own. The American Council on Education has developed a Model Policy on Awarding Credit for Extrainstitutional Learning (June 1987). It contains sample policy statements that can be adapted for local use.

Other useful sources of information are the various experiential learning organizations and your regional accrediting association. (See Appendices E and F for addresses.)

Comprehensive institutional experiential learning policies should include: (I) introductory materials such as definitions and a description of institutional commitment to assessing experiential learning; (II) and (III) separate sections on prior and sponsored experiential learning programs with regulations applicable to them; and (IV) a summary of quality assurance safeguards.

I. Introductory materials.

• A PREAMBLE describing the institution's general philosophical commitment to recognize experiential learning as a part of the overall academic service of the institution.
• DEFINITIONS of experiential learning, differentiating as appropriate between prior and sponsored learning.
• A description of TYPES OF RECOGNITION granted by the institution (e.g., credit for various kinds of examination or evaluation, and advanced placement and waivers, without credit).
• Specifications of the FACULTY ROLE (e.g., stipulating that no form

of recognition for learning, experiential or traditional, is granted without review and approval by qualified faculty members).
• Differentiating as appropriate between policies for GRADUATE and those for UNDERGRADUATE programs.

II. A section on recognition of prior experiential learning.

• Any limits on AMOUNT OF CREDIT imposed either by accreditation associations or by campus regulations (including any rules imposed by individual departments or programs).
• Any provisions, local or by accrediting associations, making the recording of prior learning credit conditional on completion of a certain number of RESIDENCE CREDITS.
• Passing scores and credit amounts allowed for any EXTERNALLY DEVELOPED EXAMINATIONS that may be accepted (e.g., CLEP, Advanced Placement, ACT, etc.).
• Provisions for recognition of NON-COLLEGIATE SPONSORED INSTRUCTION, including instruction in military service programs. (Since these sources are instructor-directed classroom learning, rather than self-directed or undirected experiential learning, some institutions prefer to treat them as transfer credit and do not include this section in the comprehensive experiential learning policy. However, there is a close relationship between this subject area and the blanket credit offered in some institutions for military experience. For this reason, it is probably helpful to students and advisors to cover all of the policies in one document.)
• Procedures and limits, if any, for recognizing TRANSFER CREDIT granted for experiential learning by other institutions.
• Procedures for recording prior learning credit on the institution's own transcripts (e.g., if credit is granted for existing courses, is it recorded differently when it is granted as a result of portfolio assessment rather than by taking the course?).
• Procedures for CREDIT BY EXAMINATION, both for existing courses and for subject areas not covered by them. Included should be: grading regulations, residency status of credit earned by examination, differences (if any) between credit by examination and credit by other means of evaluation, types of examination permitted, costs, scheduling of examinations, provisions for appeal, and any other local regulations or procedures.

• Descriptions of any SPECIAL LOCAL PROGRAMS for prior learning assessment (e.g., for reentry students, or for general education or statutory requirements, etc.).

III. A section on recognition of sponsored learning.

• Differentiation as may be necessary locally among INTERNSHIPS, COOPERATIVE EDUCATION, and other FIELD EXPERIENCE LEARNING.
• GRADING regulations and procedures.
• PREREQUISITES (e.g., grade point average, major status, class level, completion of field preparation or orientation courses, learning contracts, etc.).
• AMOUNT OF CREDIT permitted.
• Methods of recording credit on TRANSCRIPT.

IV. Quality assurance: summary of criteria for recognition of experiential learning.

Faculty members, students, accrediting bodies, graduate schools, and employers all have important needs to know the criteria that the institution applies to maintain quality assurance. A summary of criteria should include clear evidence that credit is granted only for learning and not for experience *per se*, that the learning is college-level, that provisions are made to avoid duplicate credit, and that appropriate balance is maintained between theoretical and practical learning. Reference to this CAEL publication can be effective in describing institutional safeguards for quality assurance in the recognition of experiential learning.

Appendix E
Regional Accrediting Associations
and Commissions

**NEW ENGLAND ASSOCIATION OF SCHOOLS
AND COLLEGES**
(Connecticut, Maine, Massachusetts, New Hampshire, Rhode
Island, Vermont)

Sanborn House
15 High Street
Winchester, Massachusetts 01890   (617) 729-6762

SOUTHERN ASSOCIATION OF COLLEGES AND SCHOOLS
(Alabama, Florida, Georgia, Kentucky, Louisiana, Mississippi,
North Carolina, South Carolina, Tennessee, Texas, Virginia)

Commission on Colleges
1866 Southern Lane
Decatur, Georgia 30033-4097   (404) 329-6500

NORTHWEST ASSOCIATION OF SCHOOLS AND COLLEGES
(Alaska, Idaho, Montana, Nevada, Oregon, Utah, Washington)

Commission on Colleges
3700-B University Way, N.E.
Seattle, Washington 98105   (206) 543-0195

**NORTH CENTRAL ASSOCIATION OF COLLEGES
AND SCHOOLS**
(Arizona, Arkansas, Colorado, Illinois, Indiana, Iowa, Kansas,
Michigan, Minnesota, Missouri, Nebraska, North Dakota, Ohio,
Oklahoma, South Dakota, West Virginia, Wisconsin, Wyoming)

Commission on Institutions of Higher Education
159 North Dearborn Street
Chicago, Illinois 60601   (800) 621-7440

WESTERN ASSOCIATION OF SCHOOLS AND COLLEGES
(California, Hawaii, American Samoa, Guam, and the
Commonwealth of the Northern Marianas)

Accrediting Commission for Senior Colleges
    and Universities
c/o Mills College, Box 9990
Oakland, California 94613   (415) 632-5000

MIDDLE STATES ASSOCIATION OF COLLEGES
AND SCHOOLS
(Delaware, District of Columbia, Maryland, New Jersey, New
York, Pennsylvania, Puerto Rico, Virgin Islands)

Commission on Higher Education
3624 Market Street
Philadelphia, Pennsylvania 19104   (215) 662-5606

Appendix F
Experiential Learning Organizations

CAEL, The Council for Adult and Experiential Learning

226 South 16th Street
Philadelphia, Pennsylvania 19102   (215) 790-9010

CEA, Cooperative Education Association

655 Fifteenth N.W.
Washington, D.C. 20005   (202) 639-4770

NSIEE, National Society for Internships and Experiential Education

3509 Haworth #207
Raleigh, North Carolina 27609   (919) 787-3263

Each of these organizations holds international, national, and regional conferences. They also provide consulting and other services, and publish resource materials.